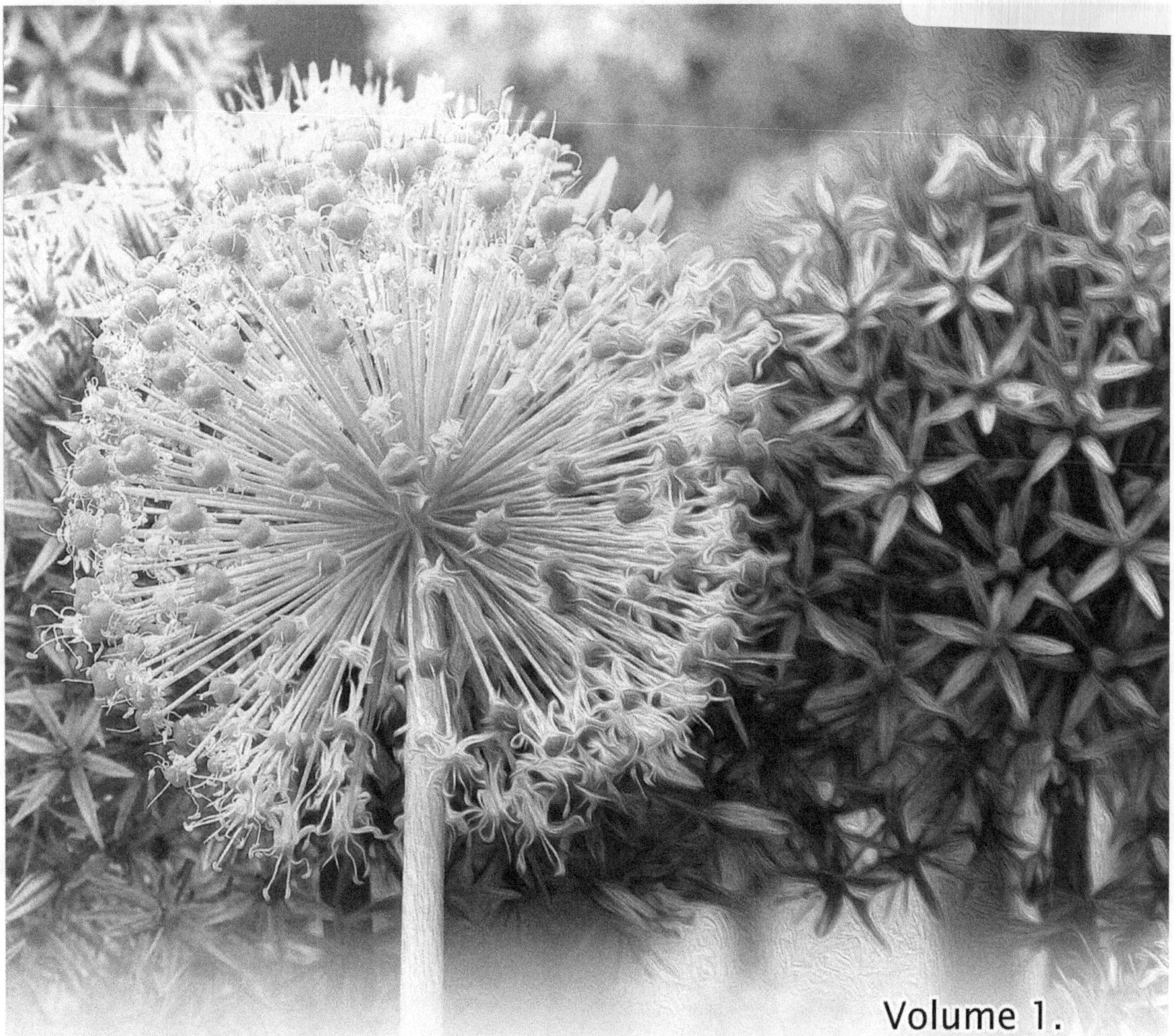

Volume 1.

BLOSSOM
STRESS RELIEF
GRAYSCALE LANDSCAPE
COLORING BOOKS

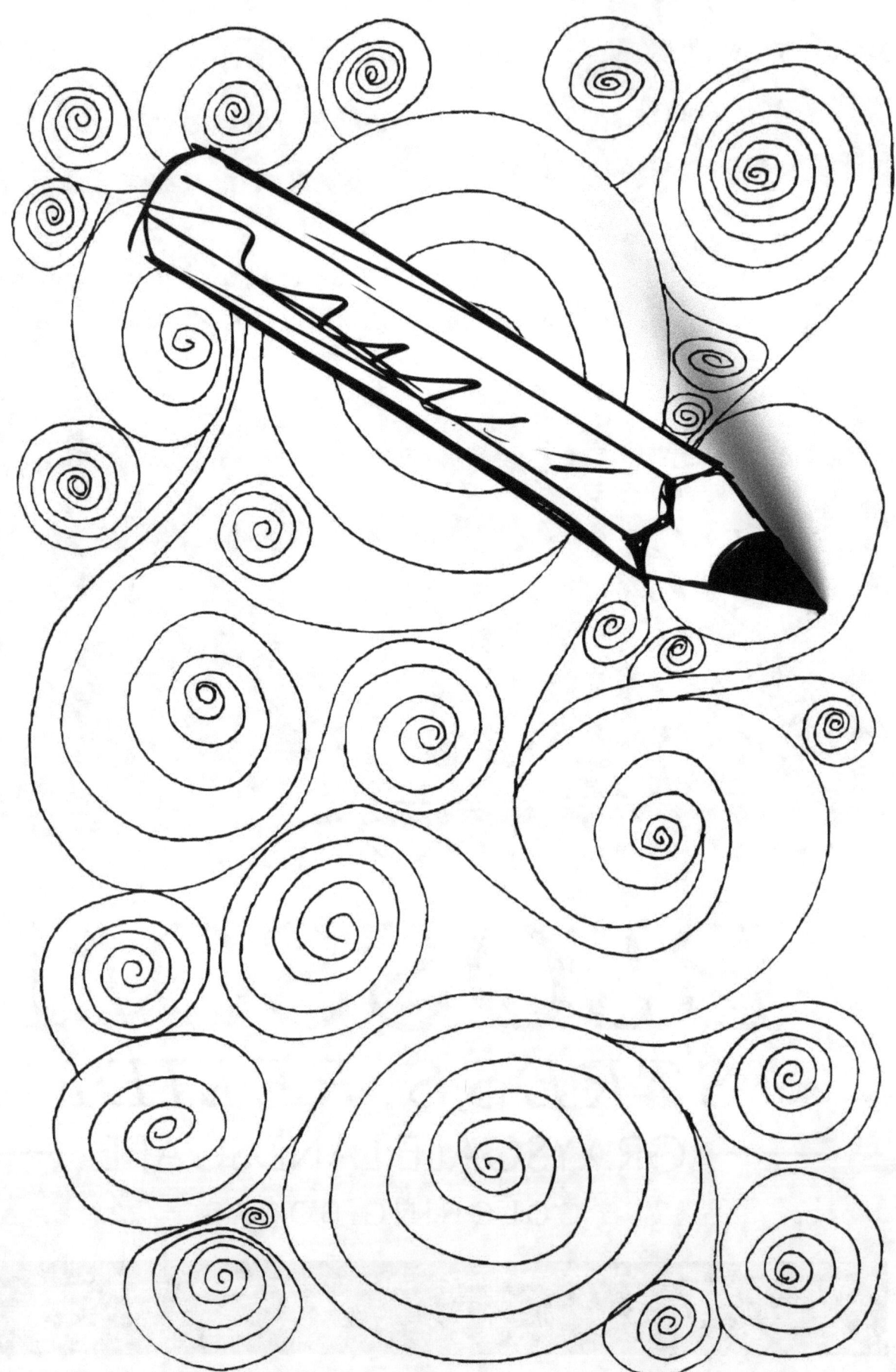

COLOR TEST PAGE

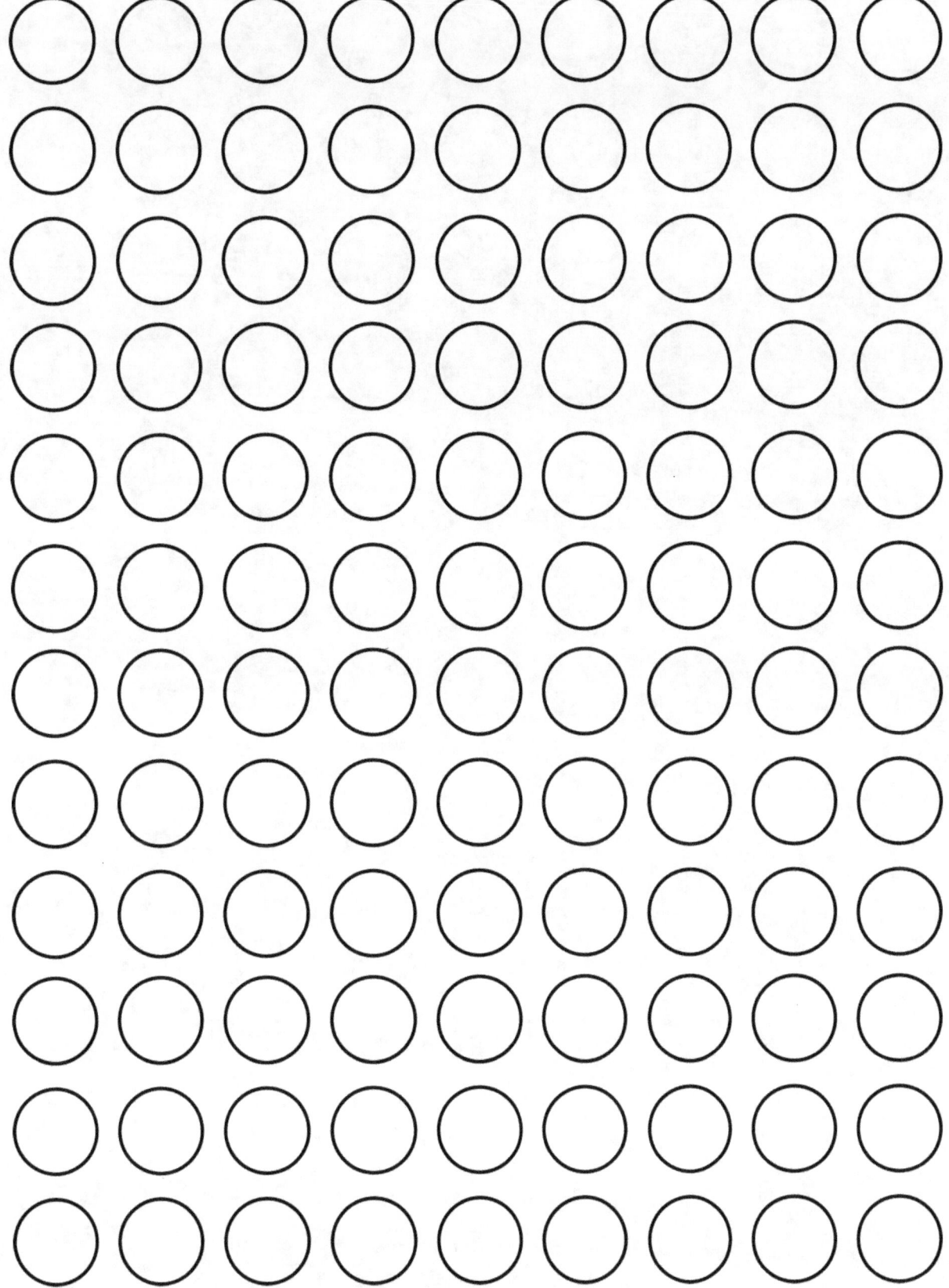

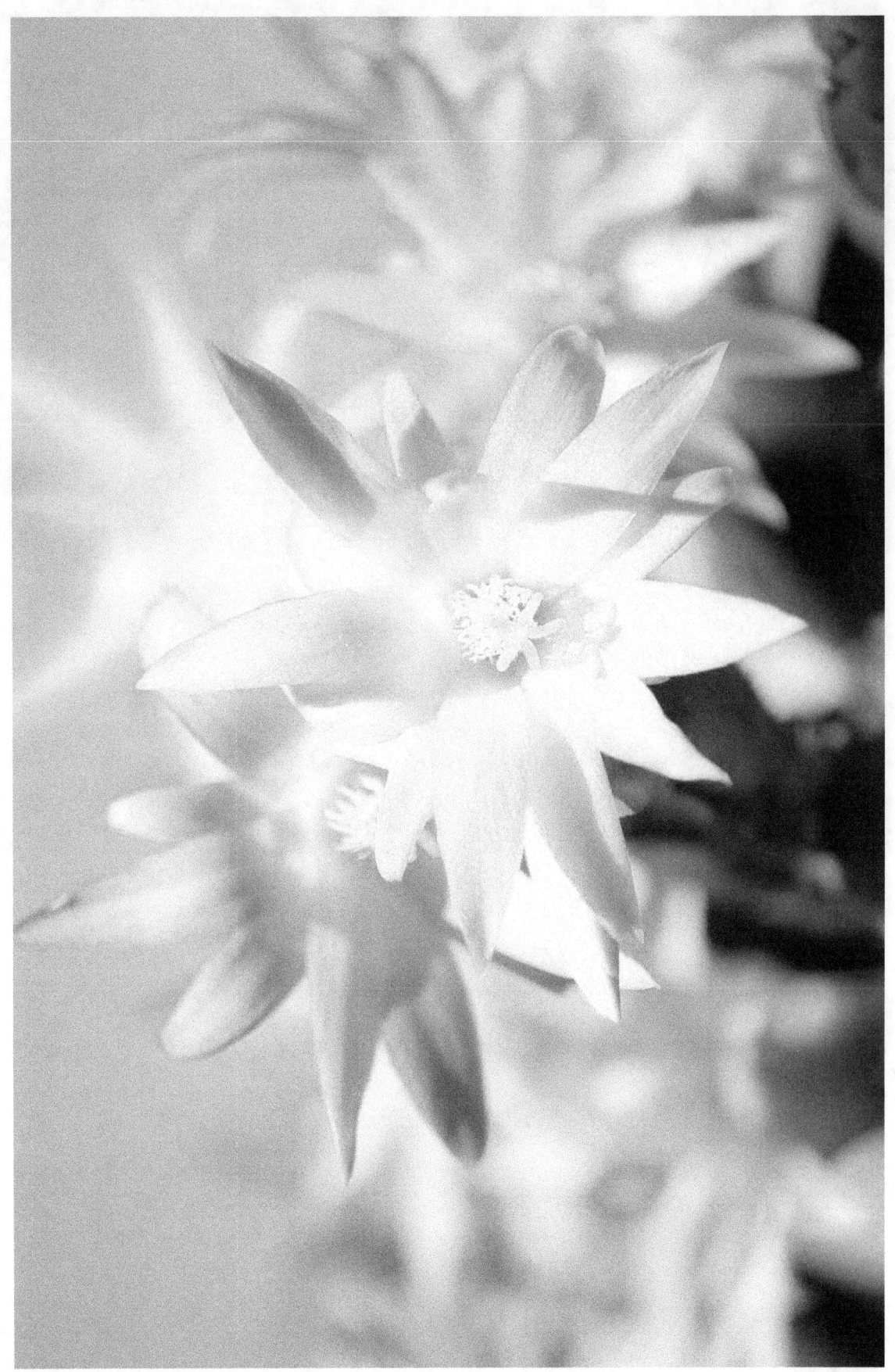

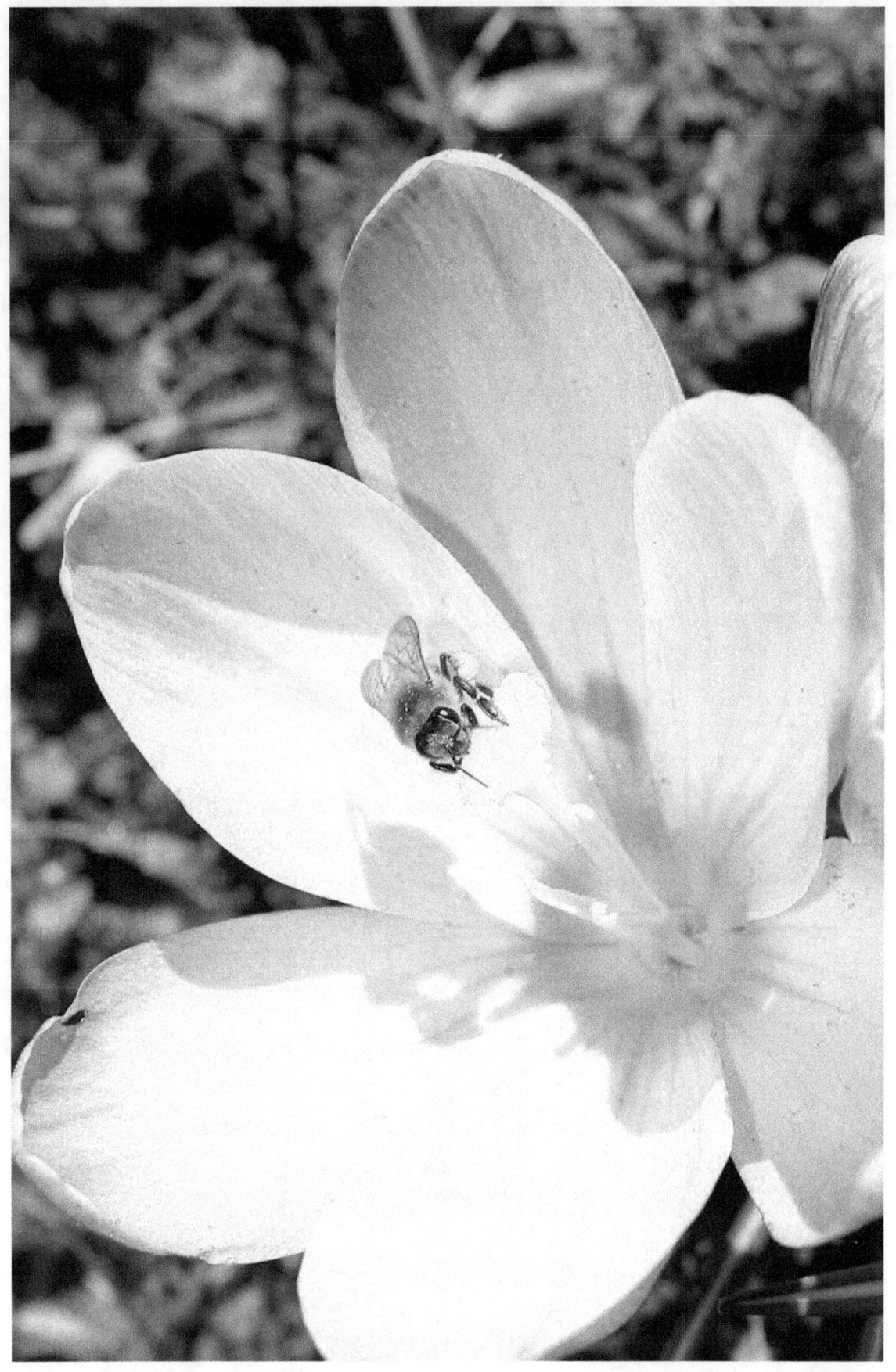

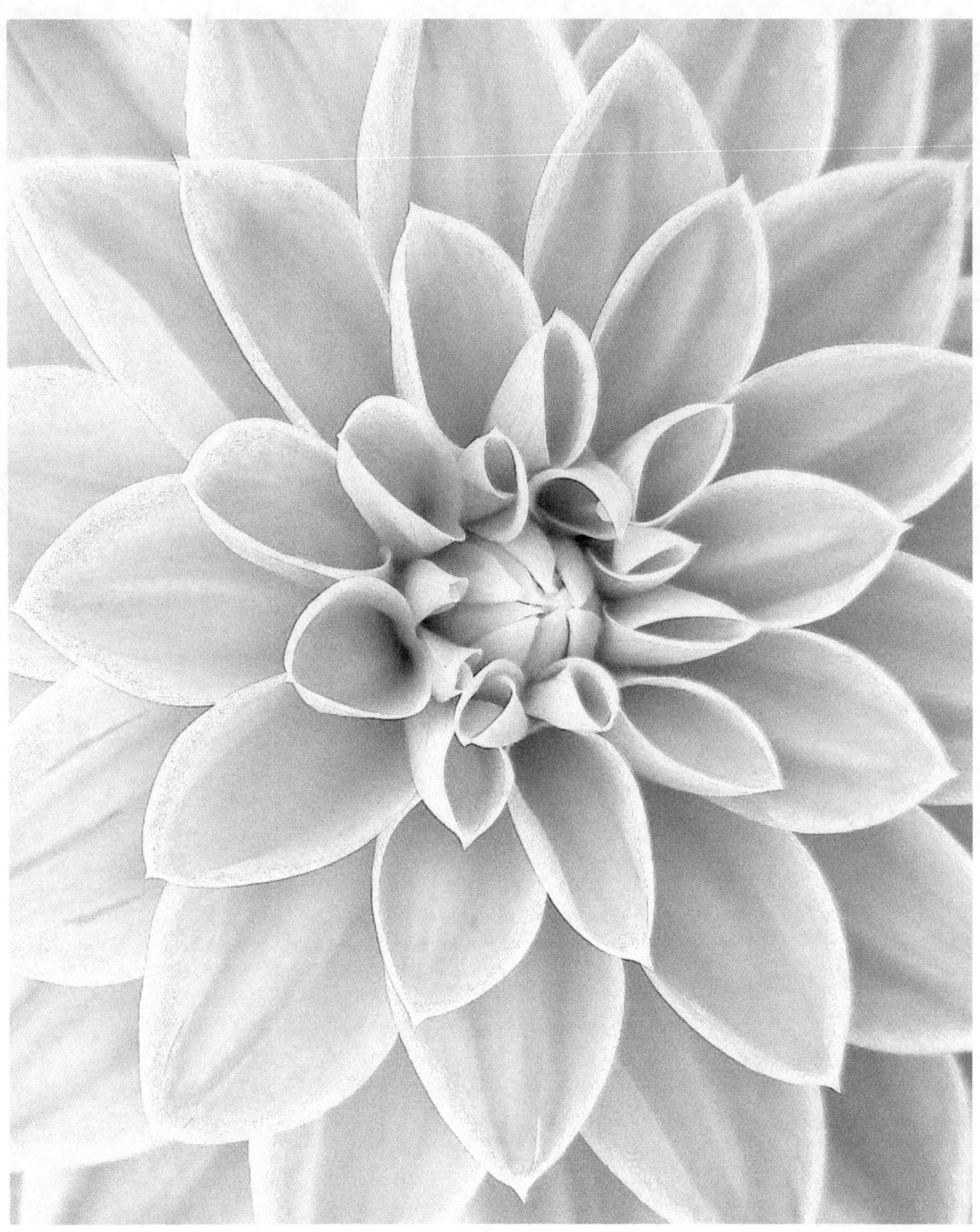

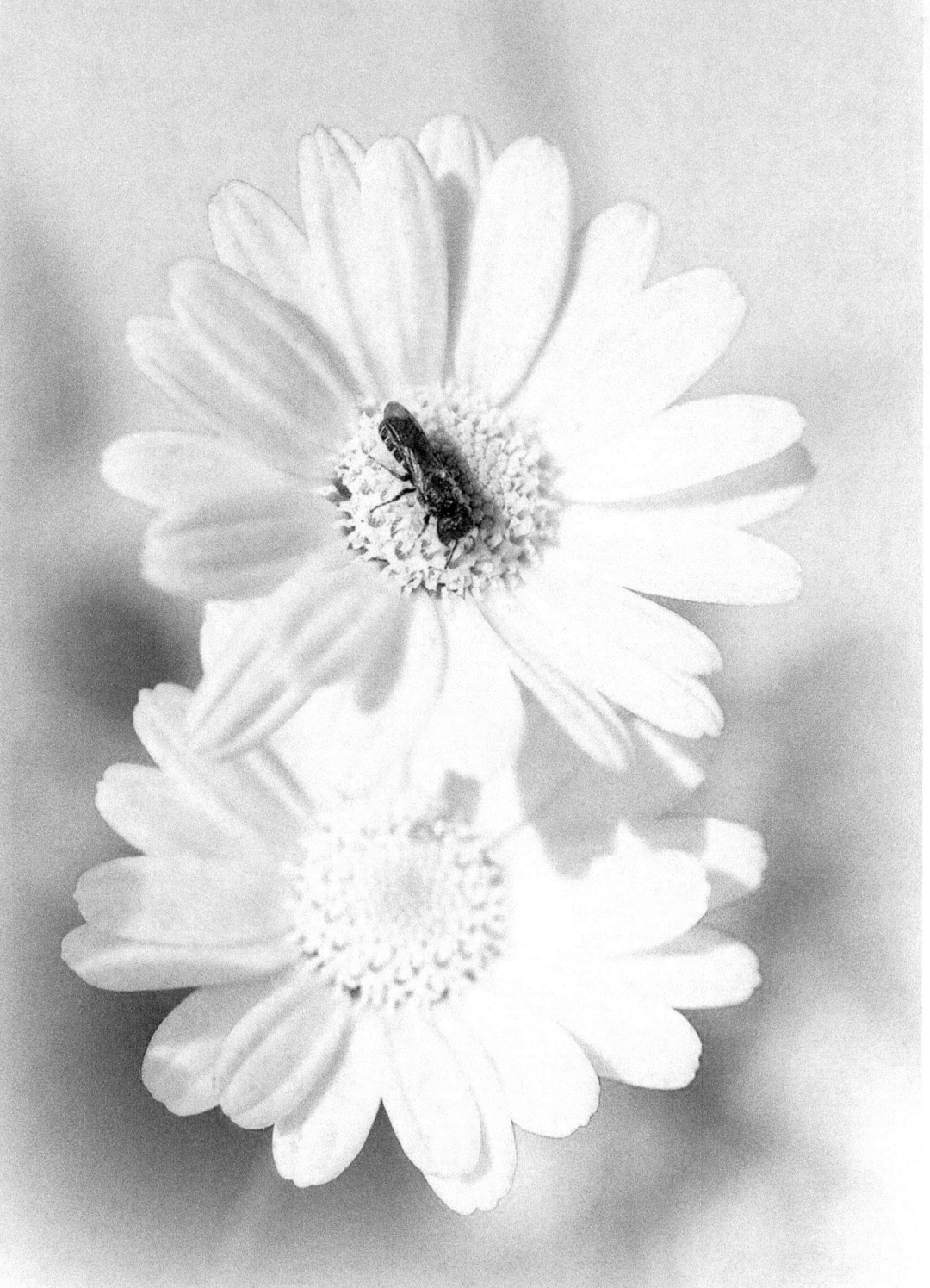

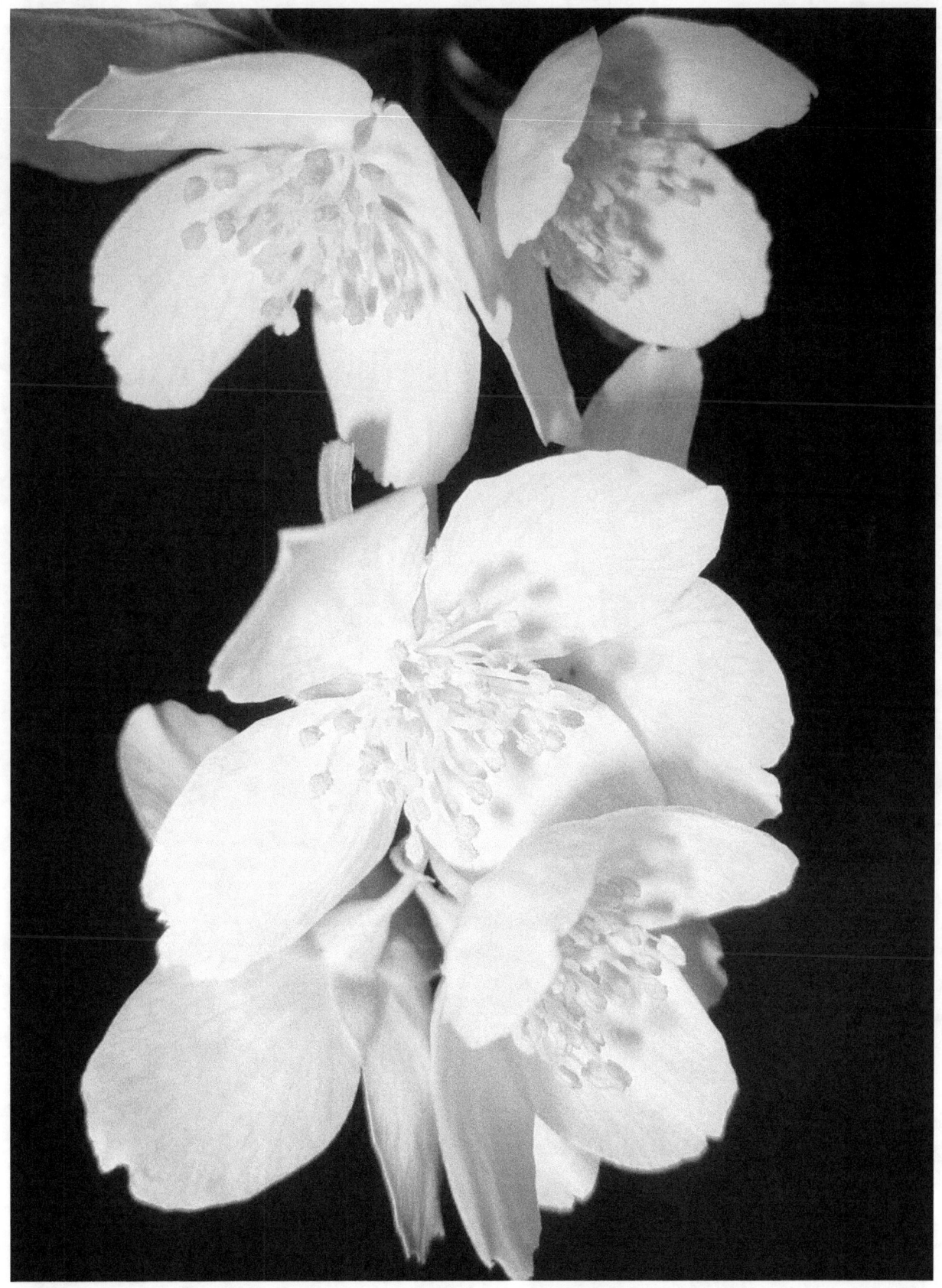

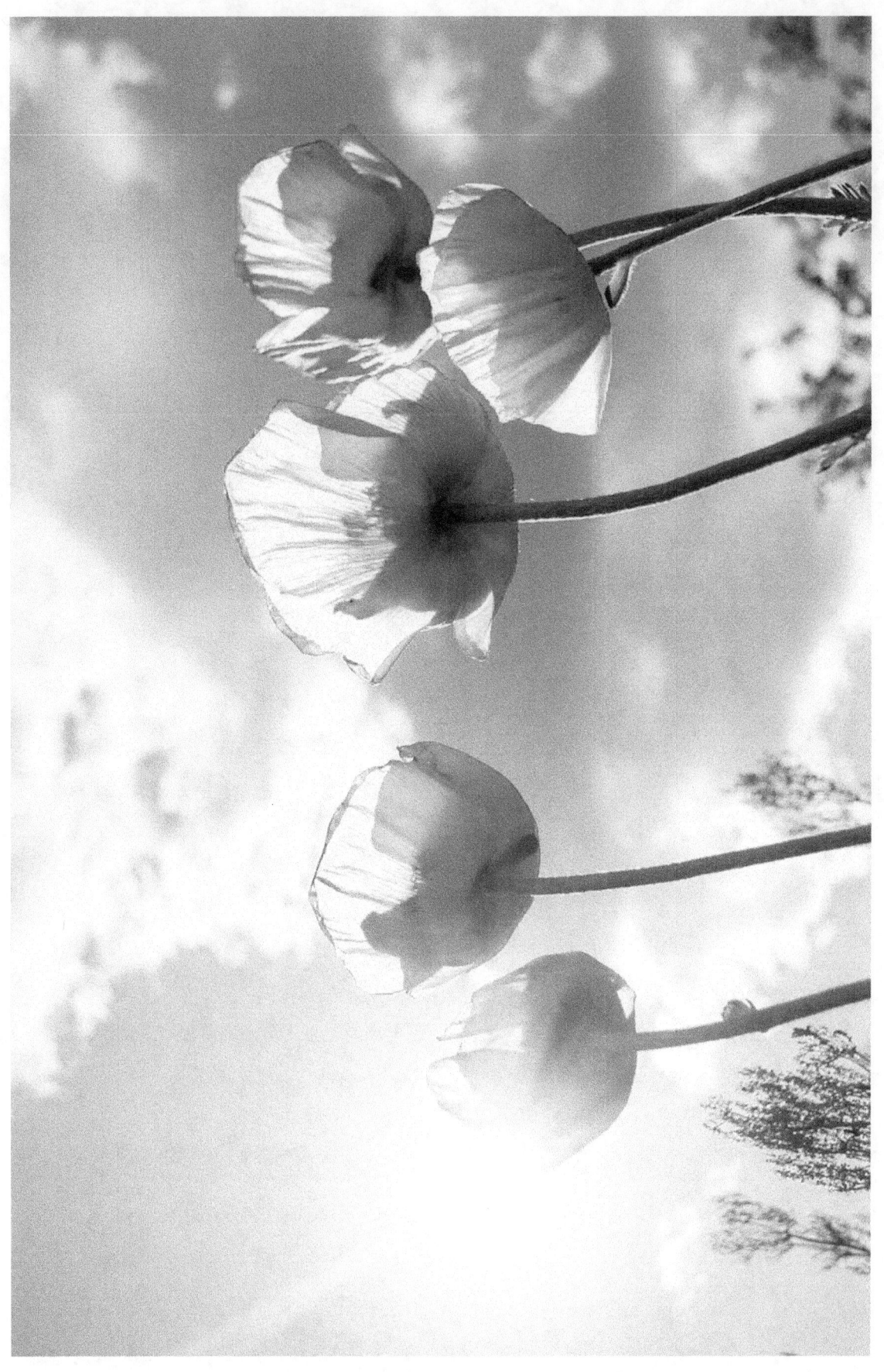

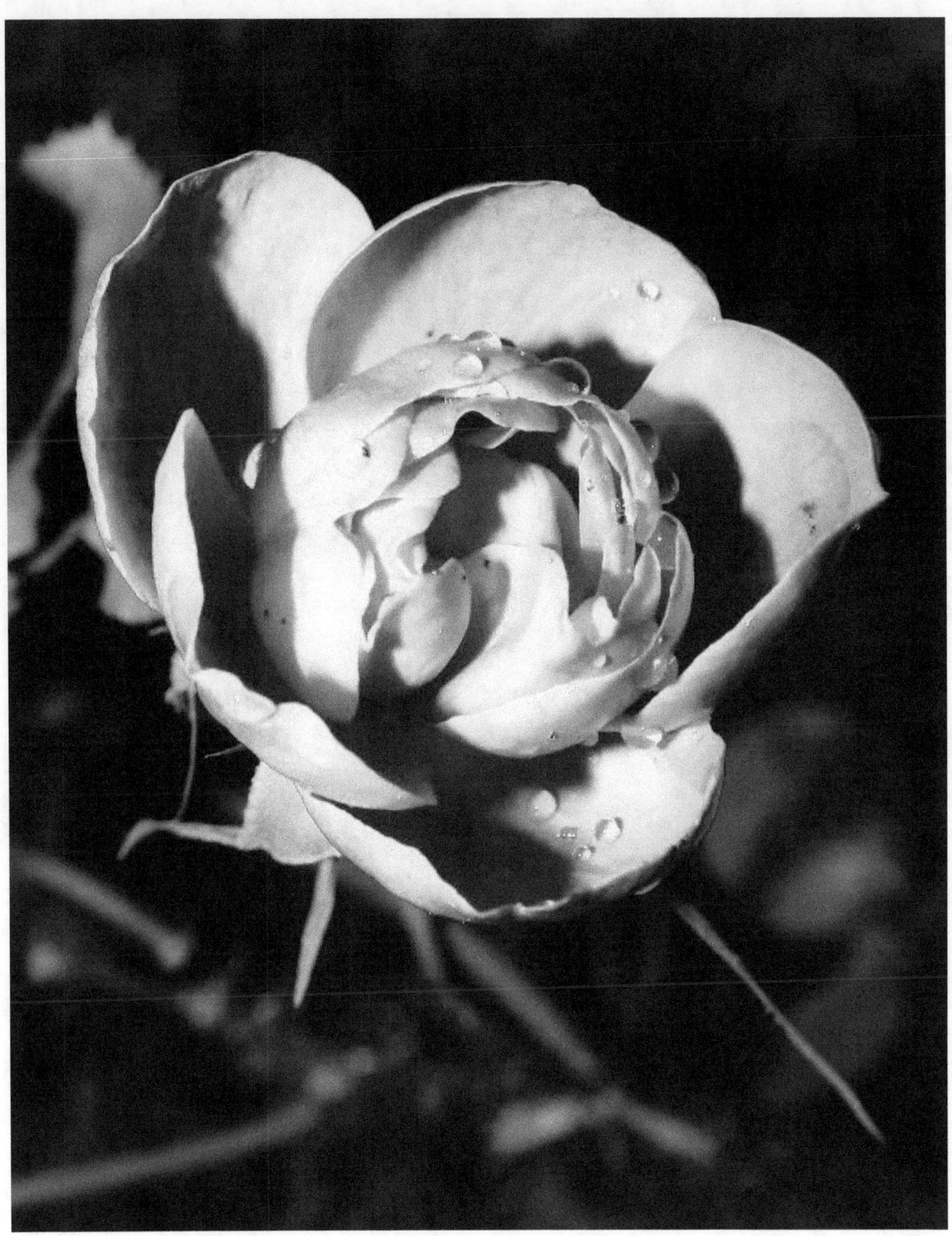

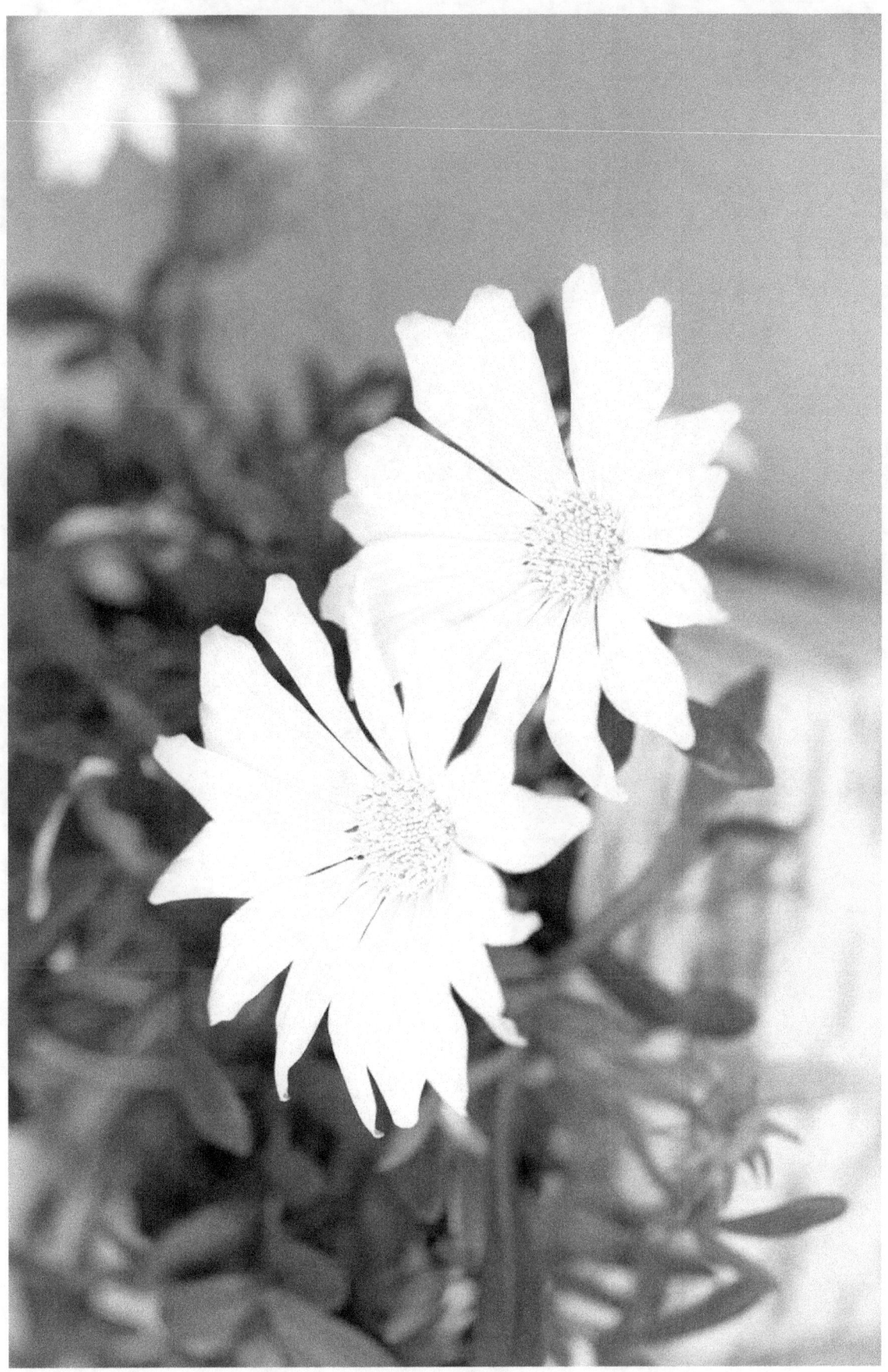

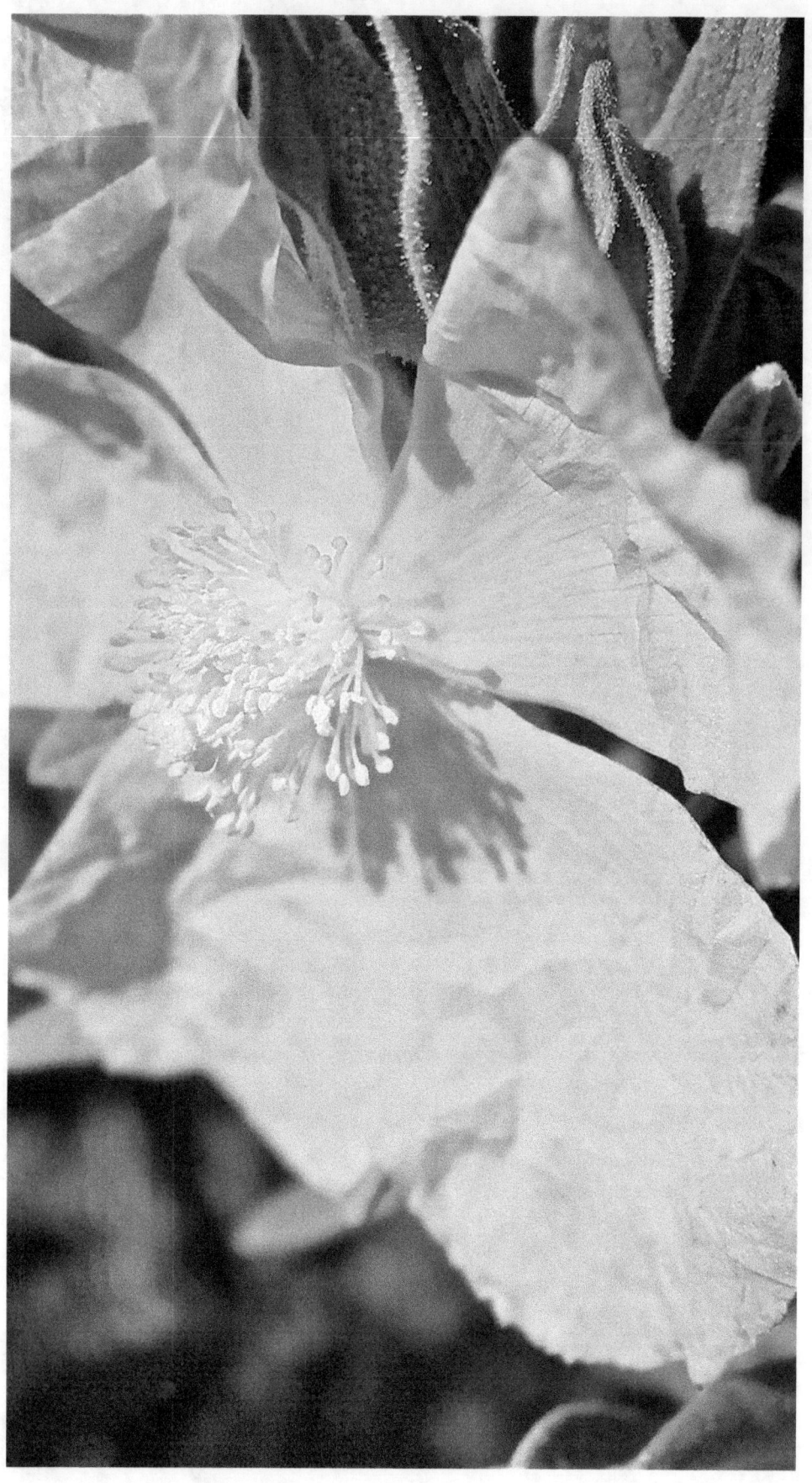

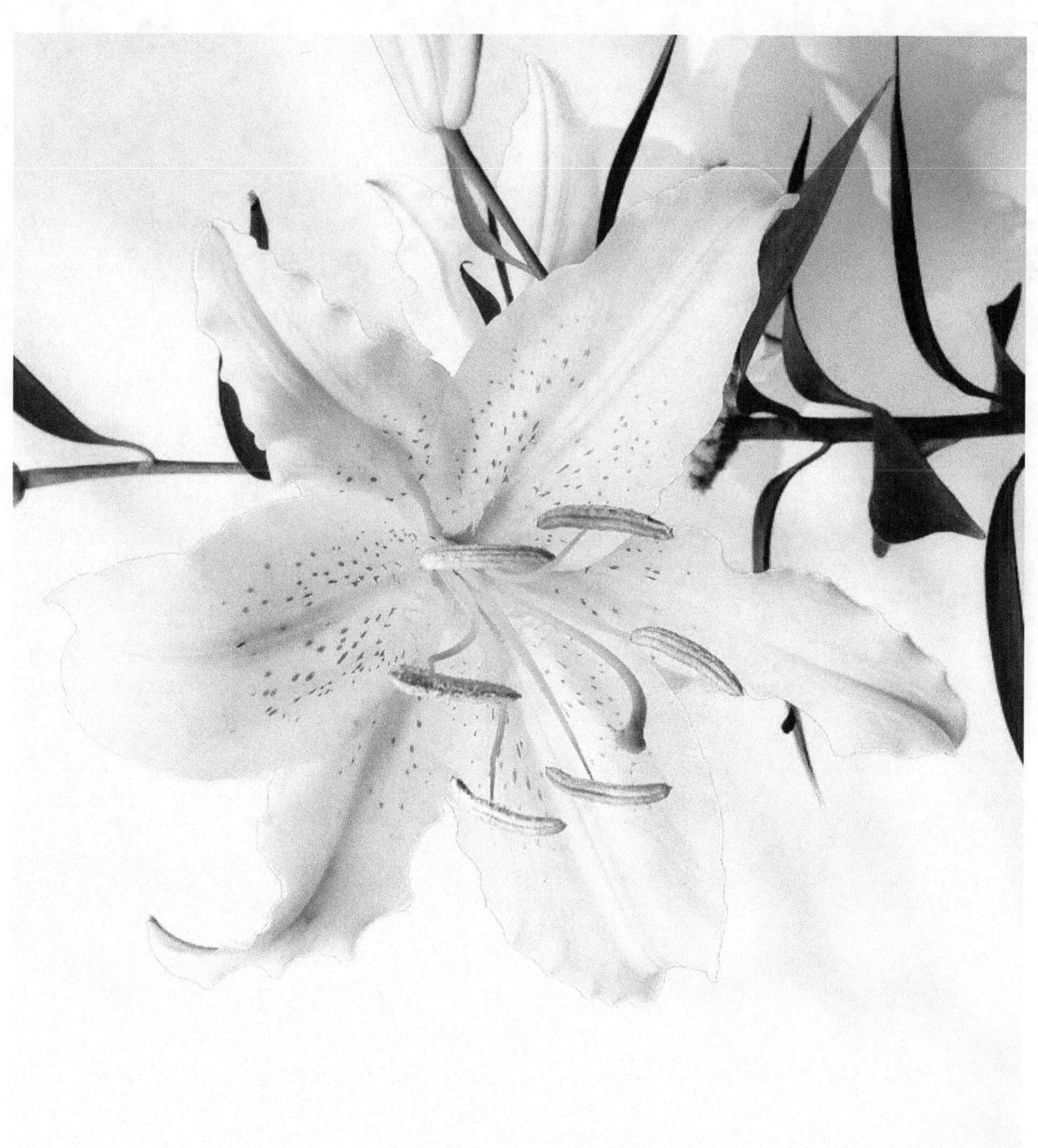

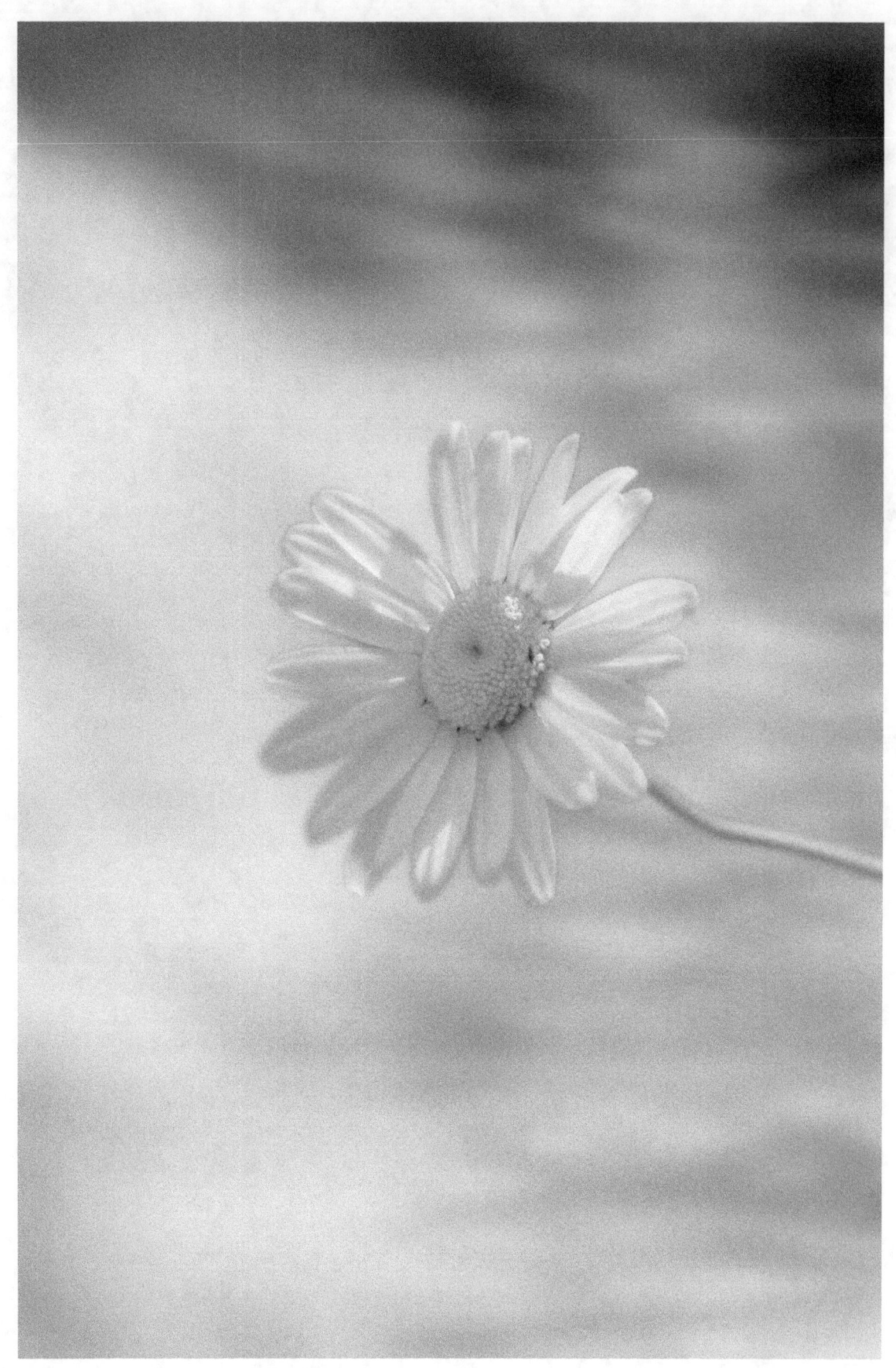

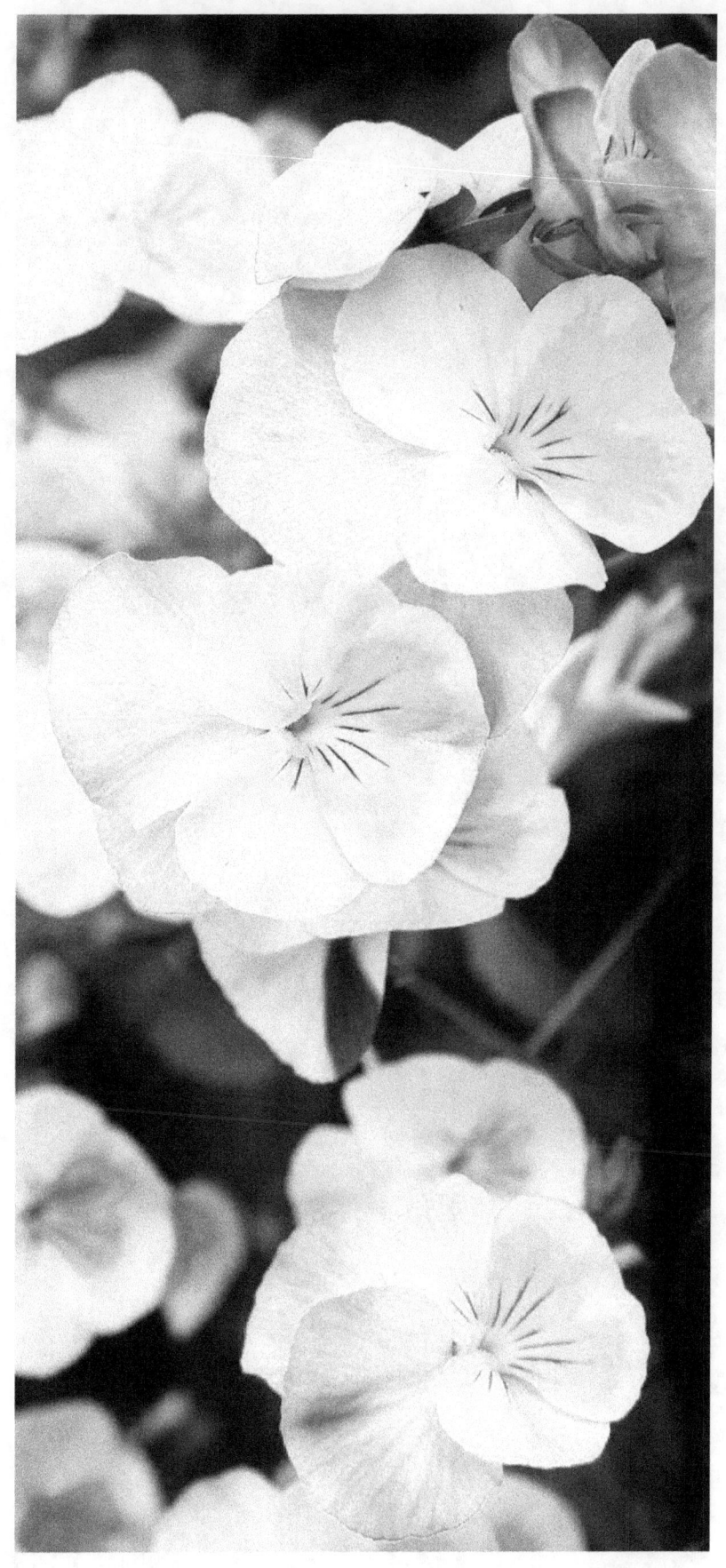

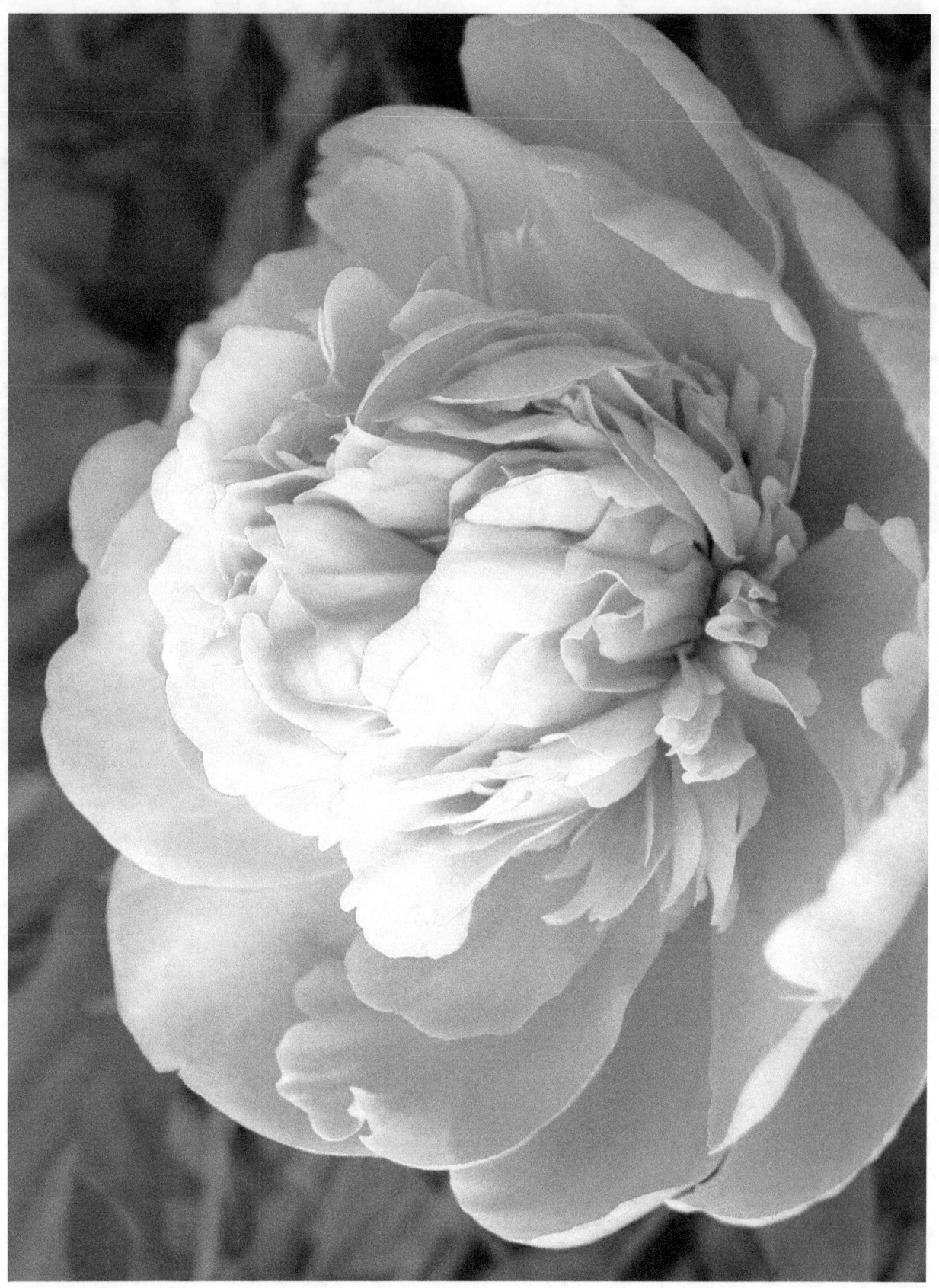

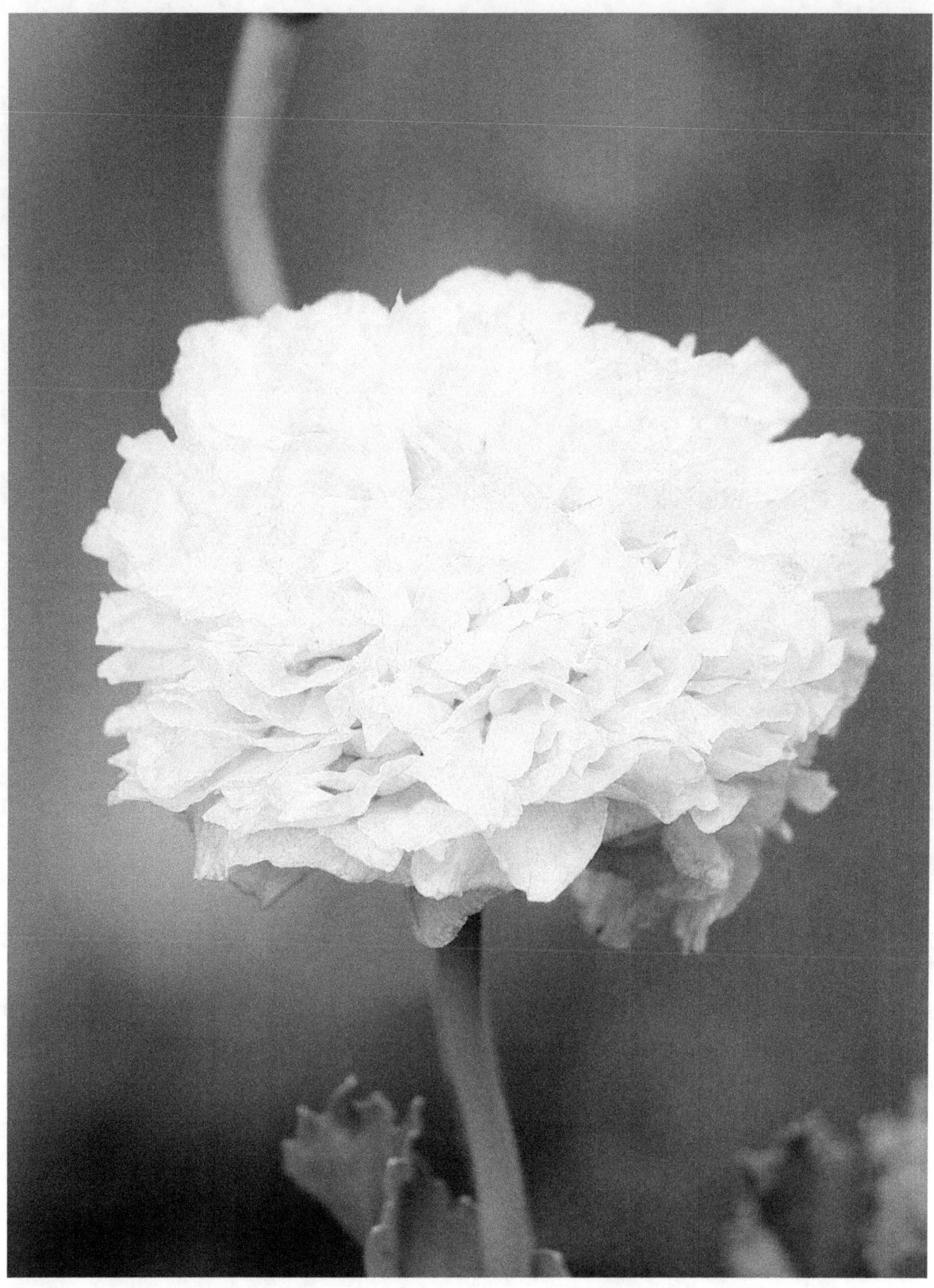

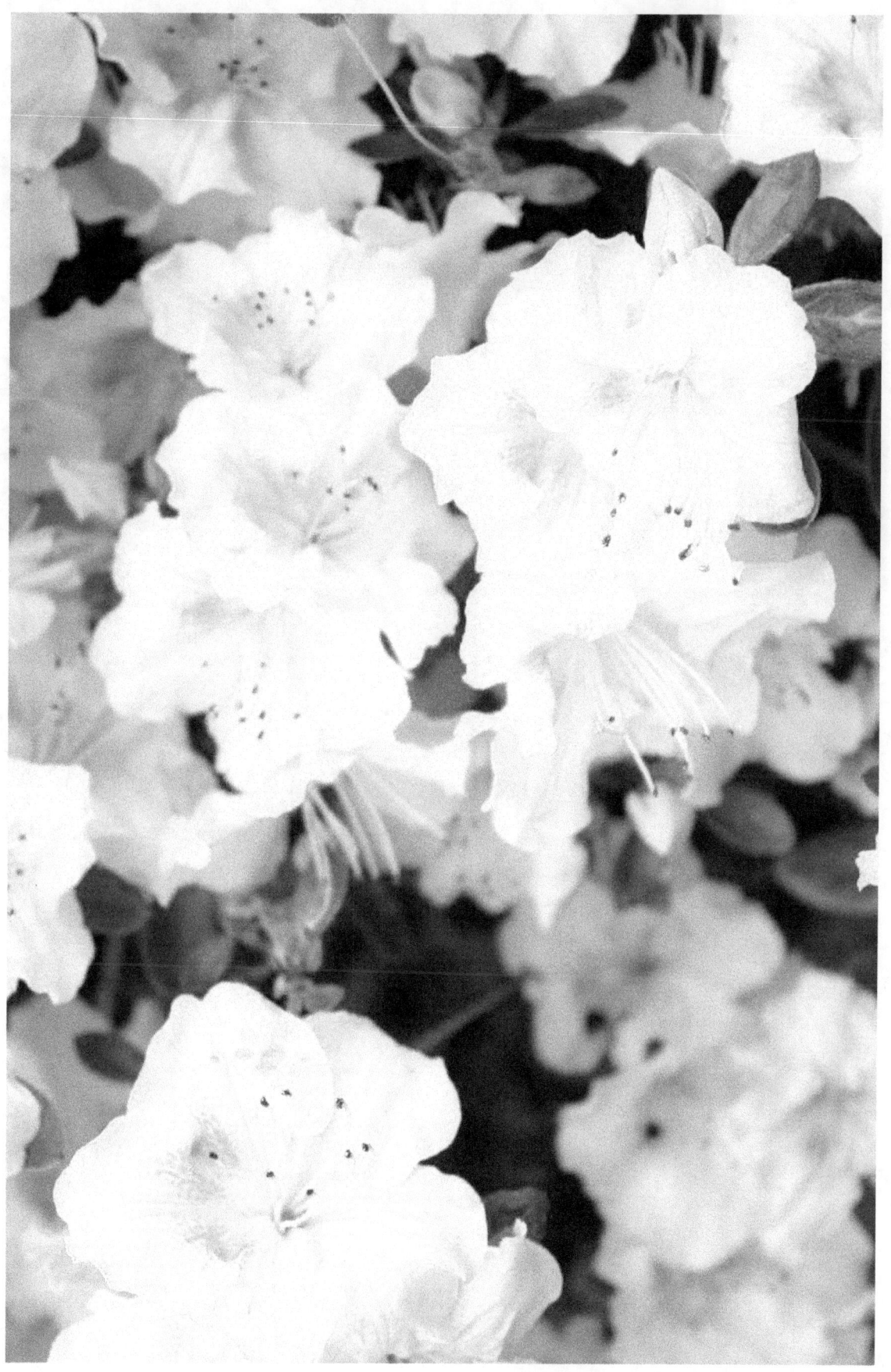

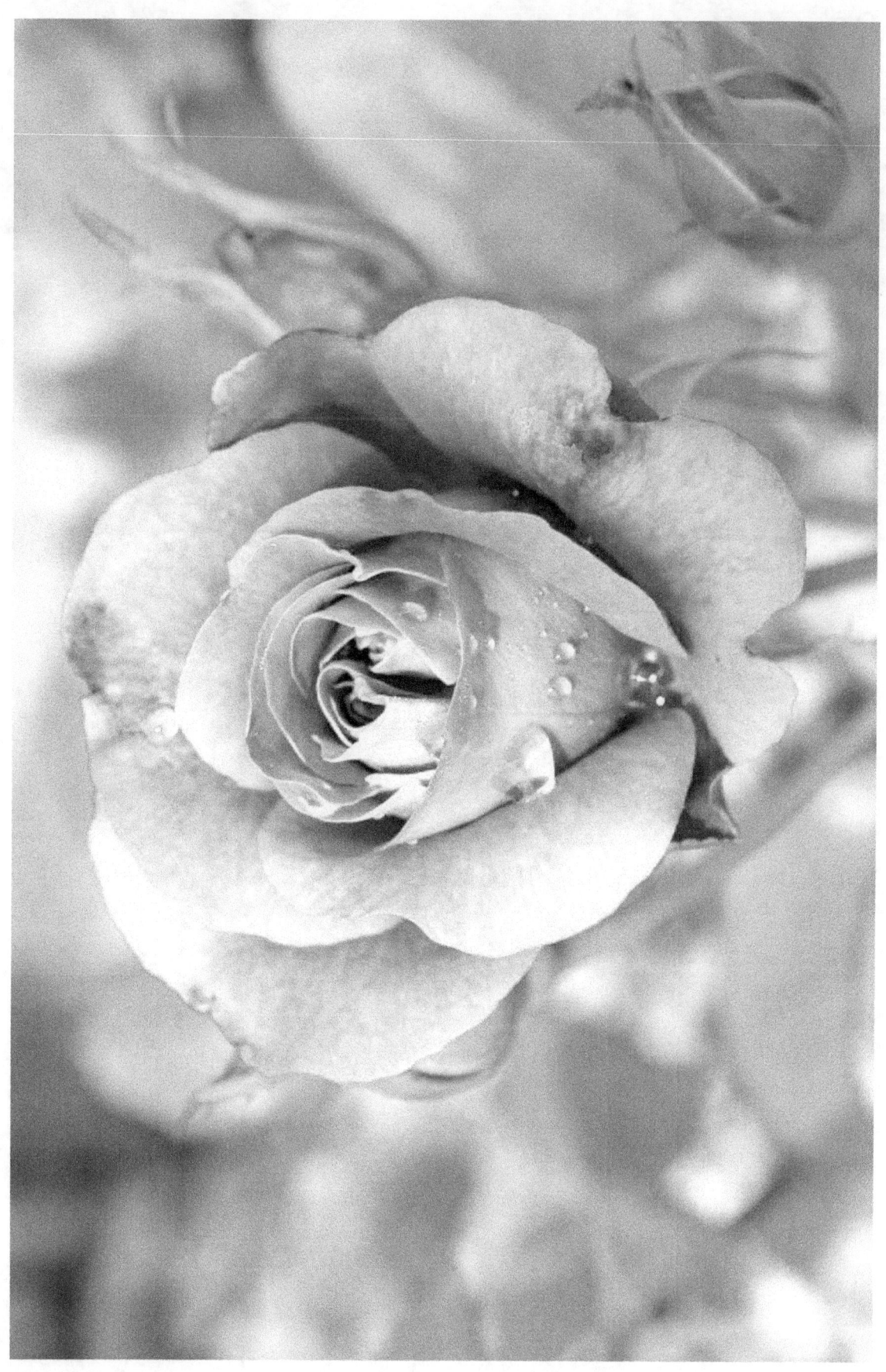

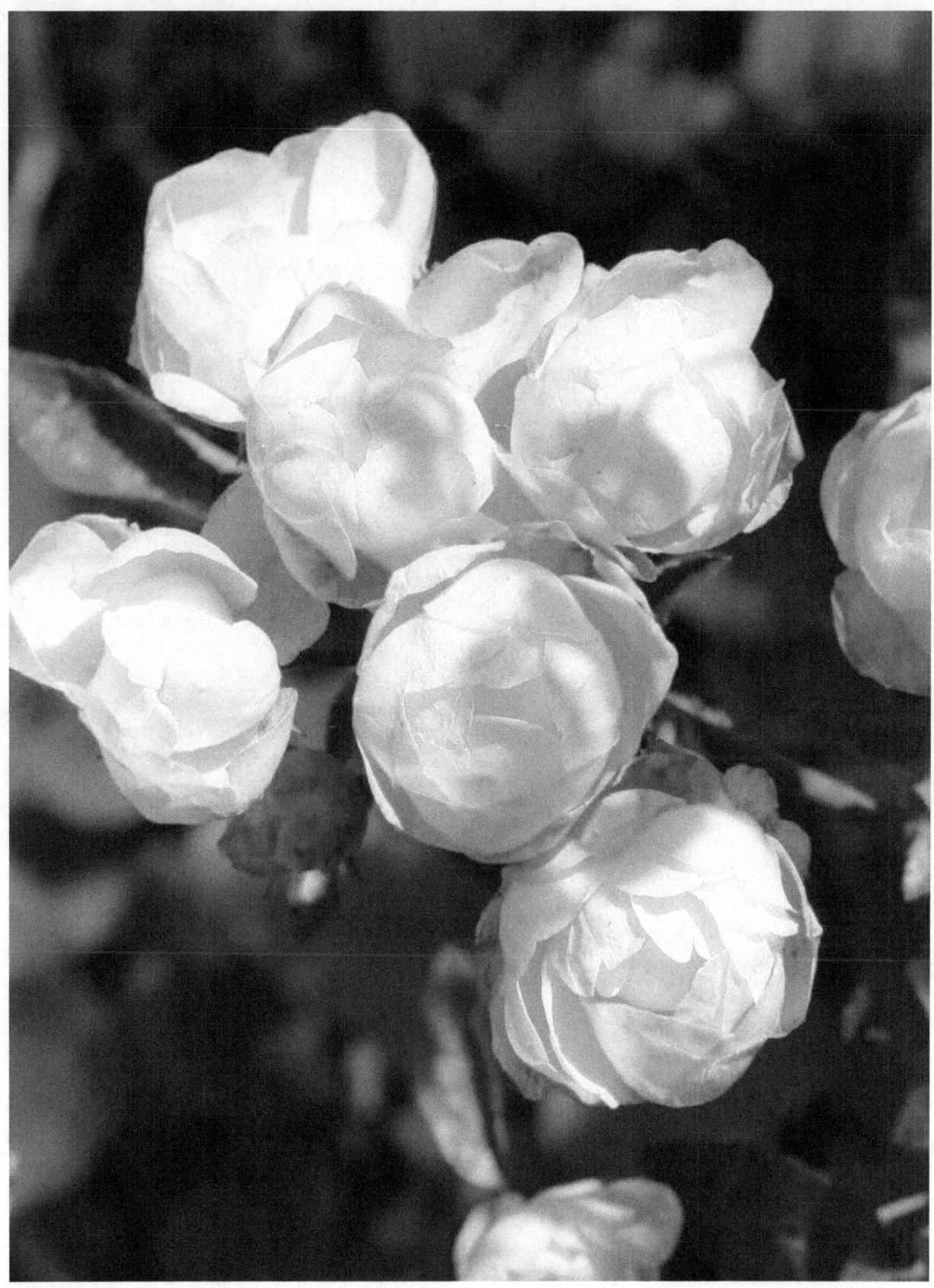

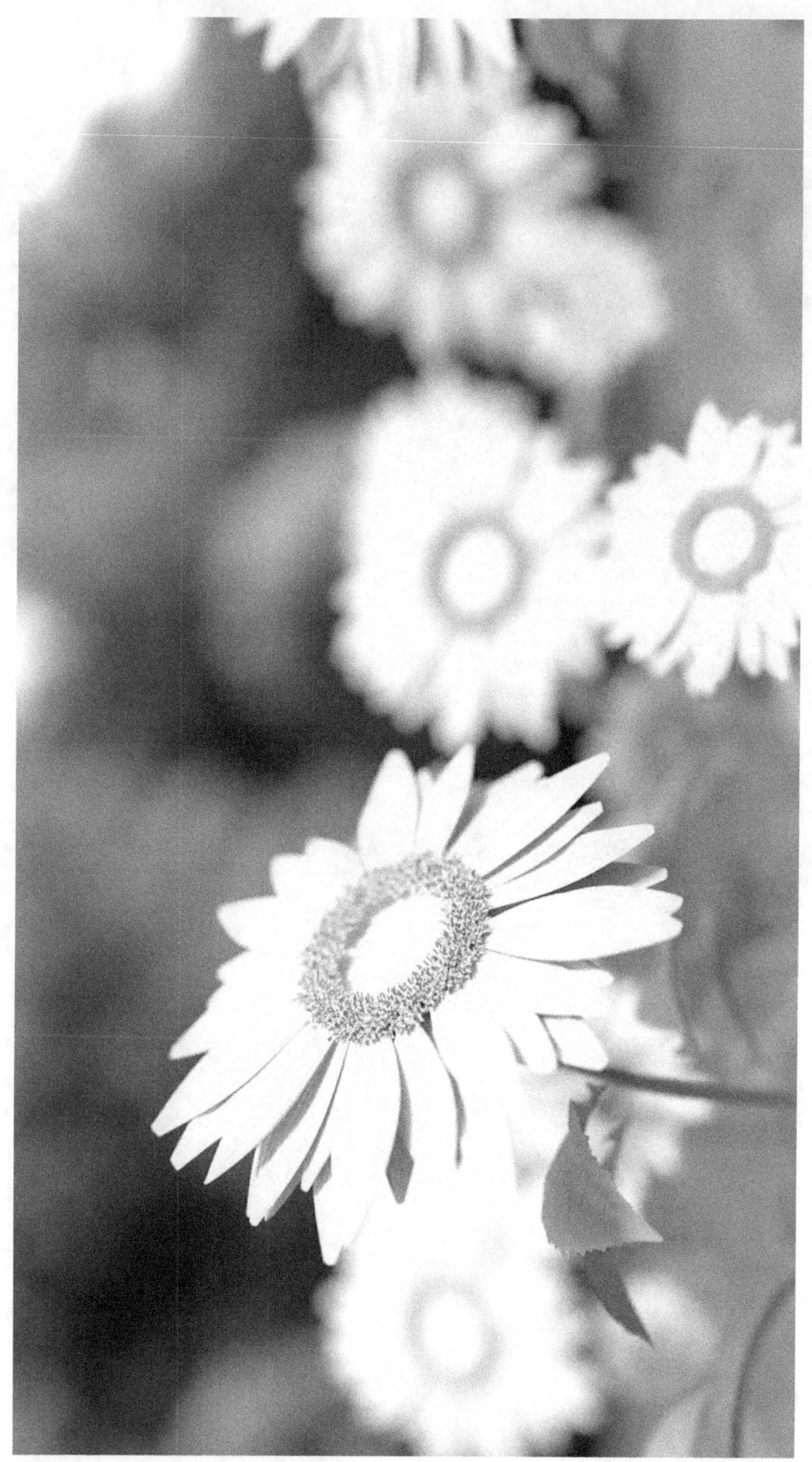

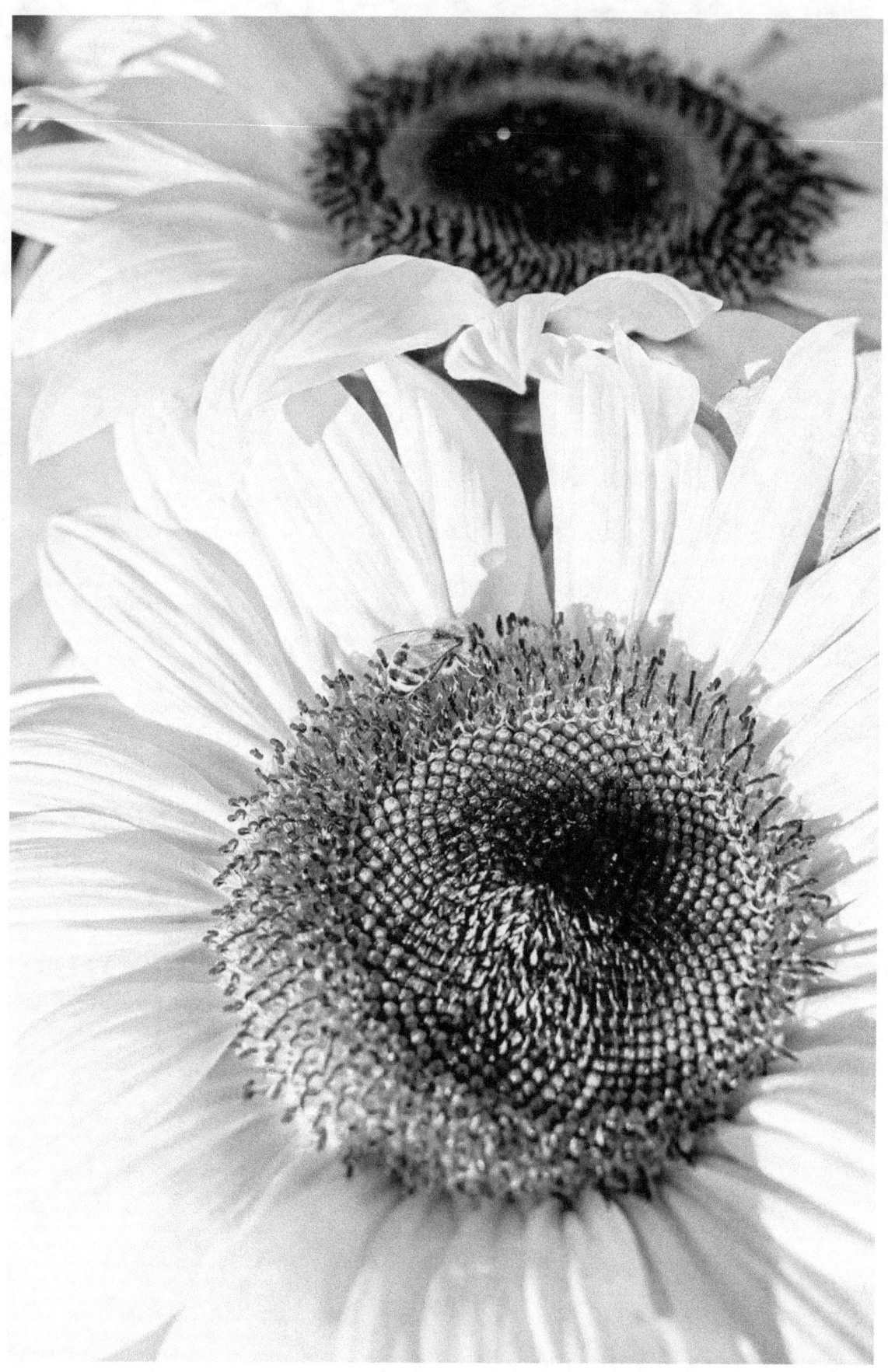

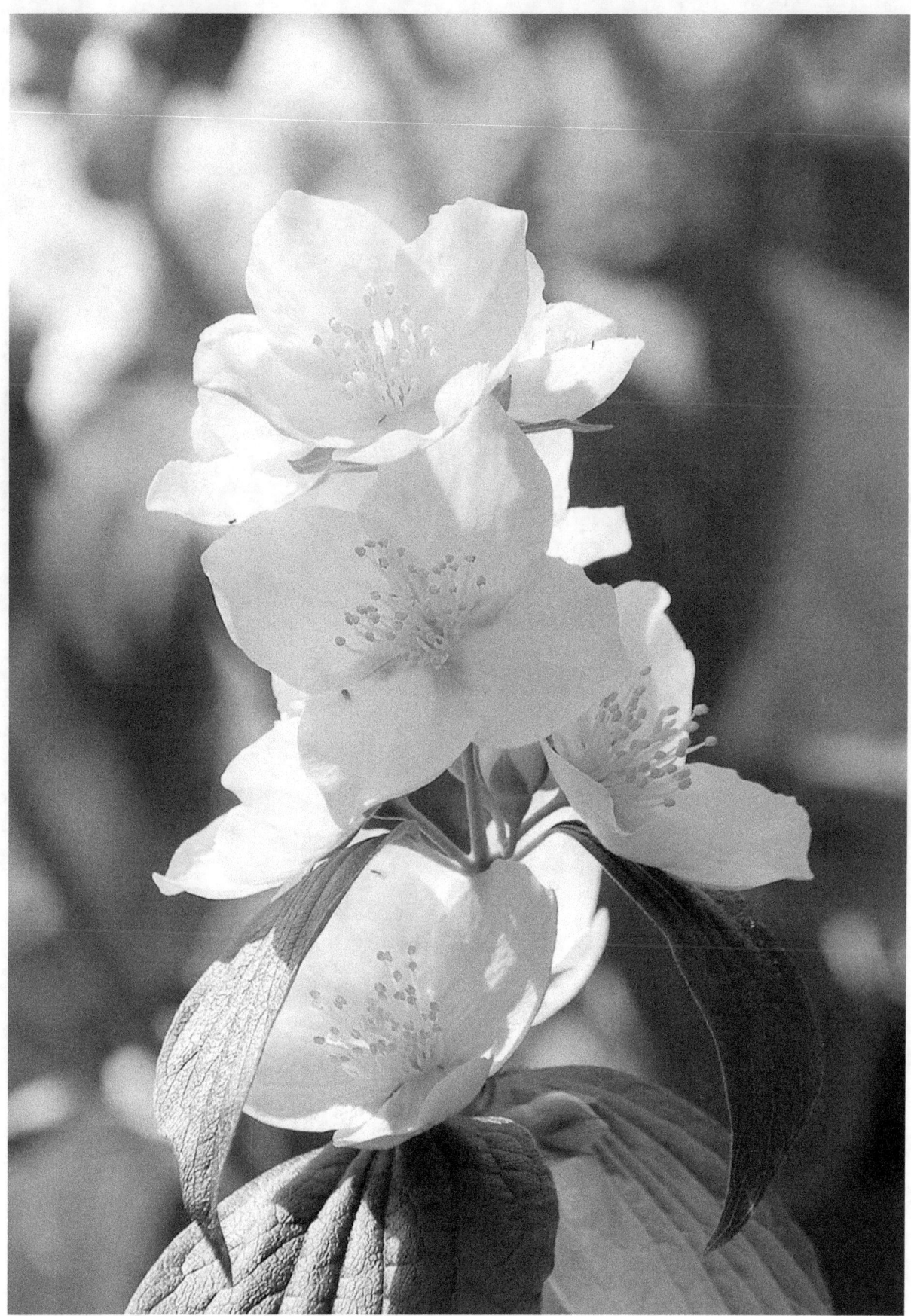

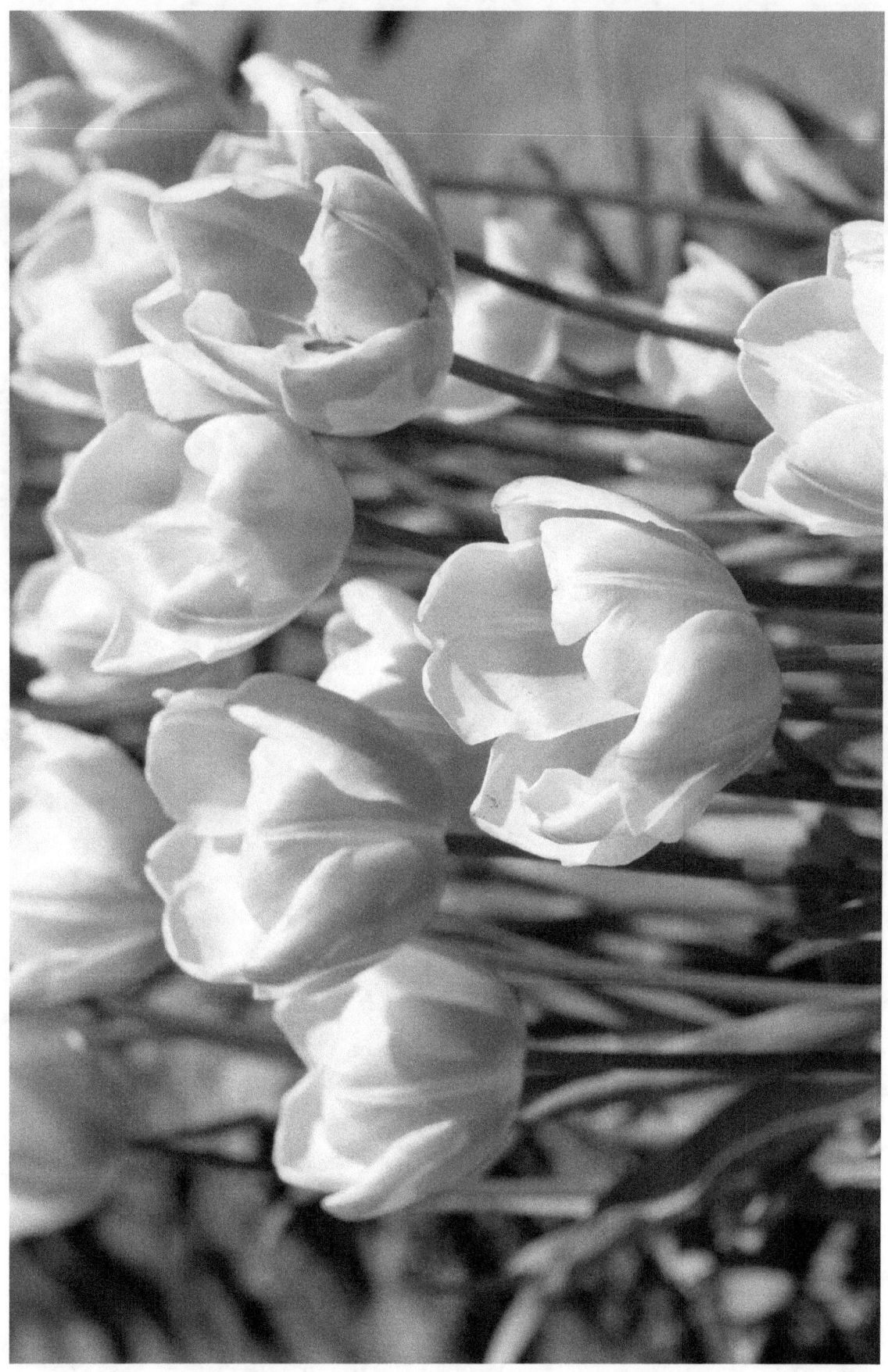

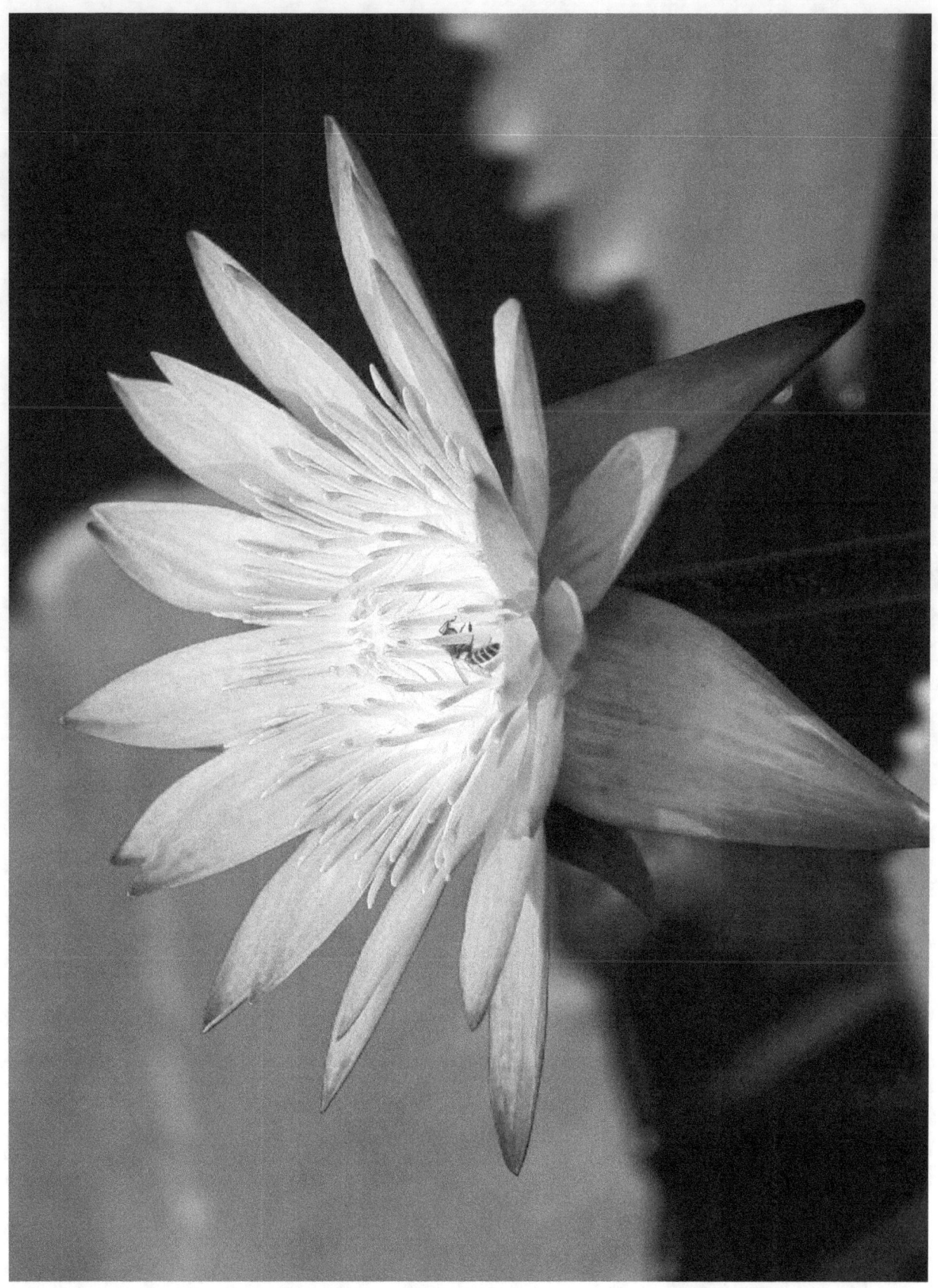

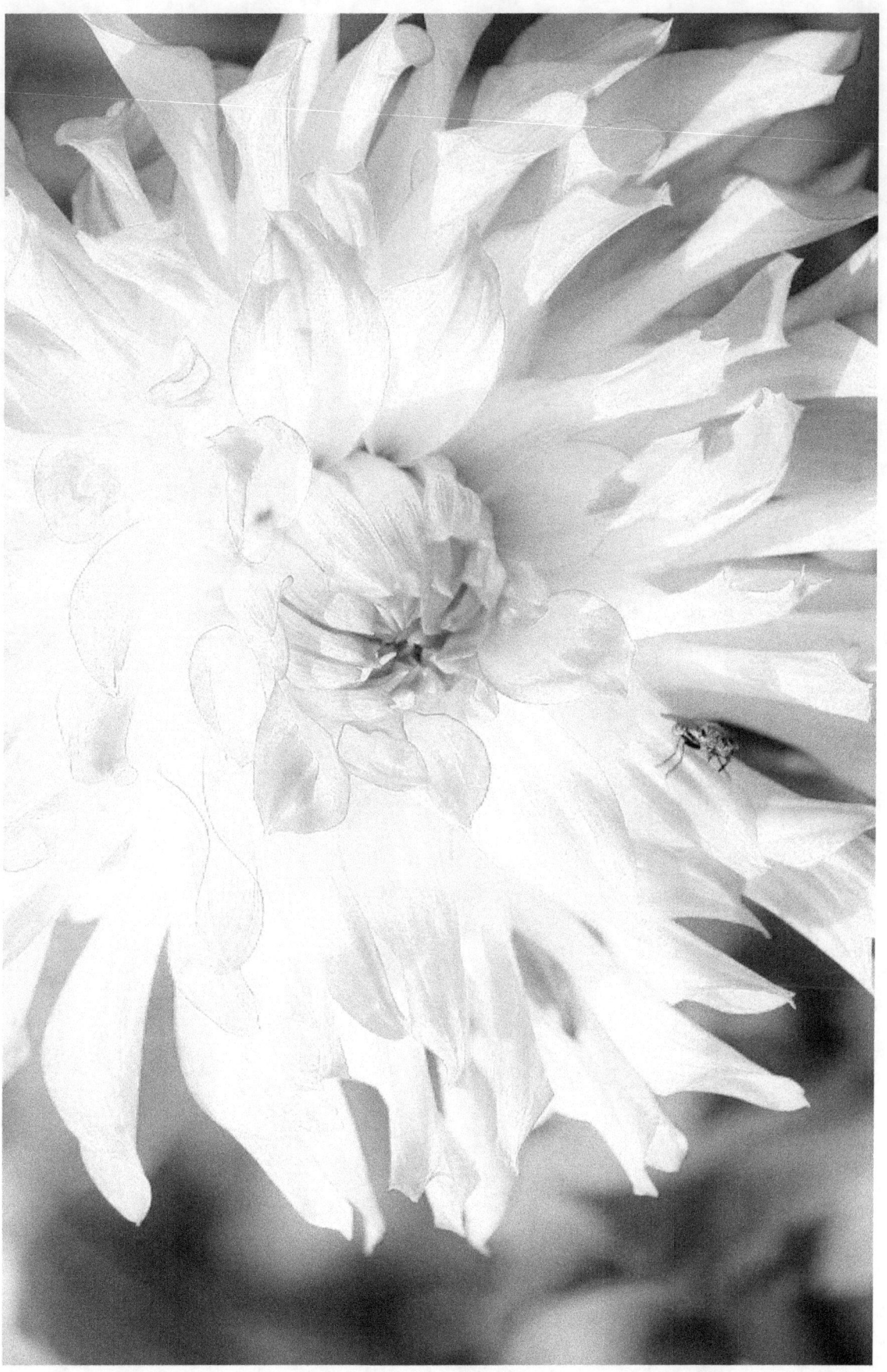

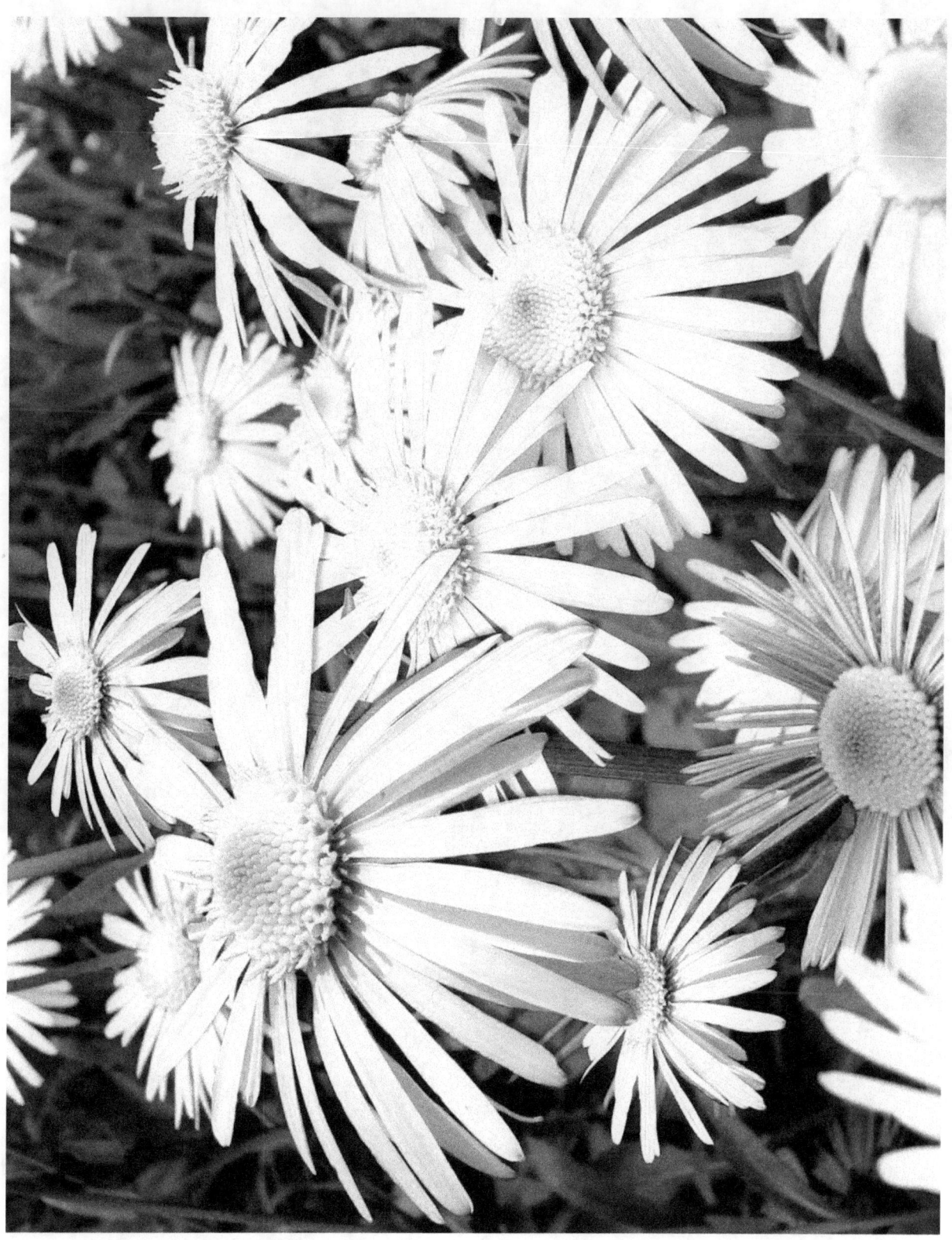

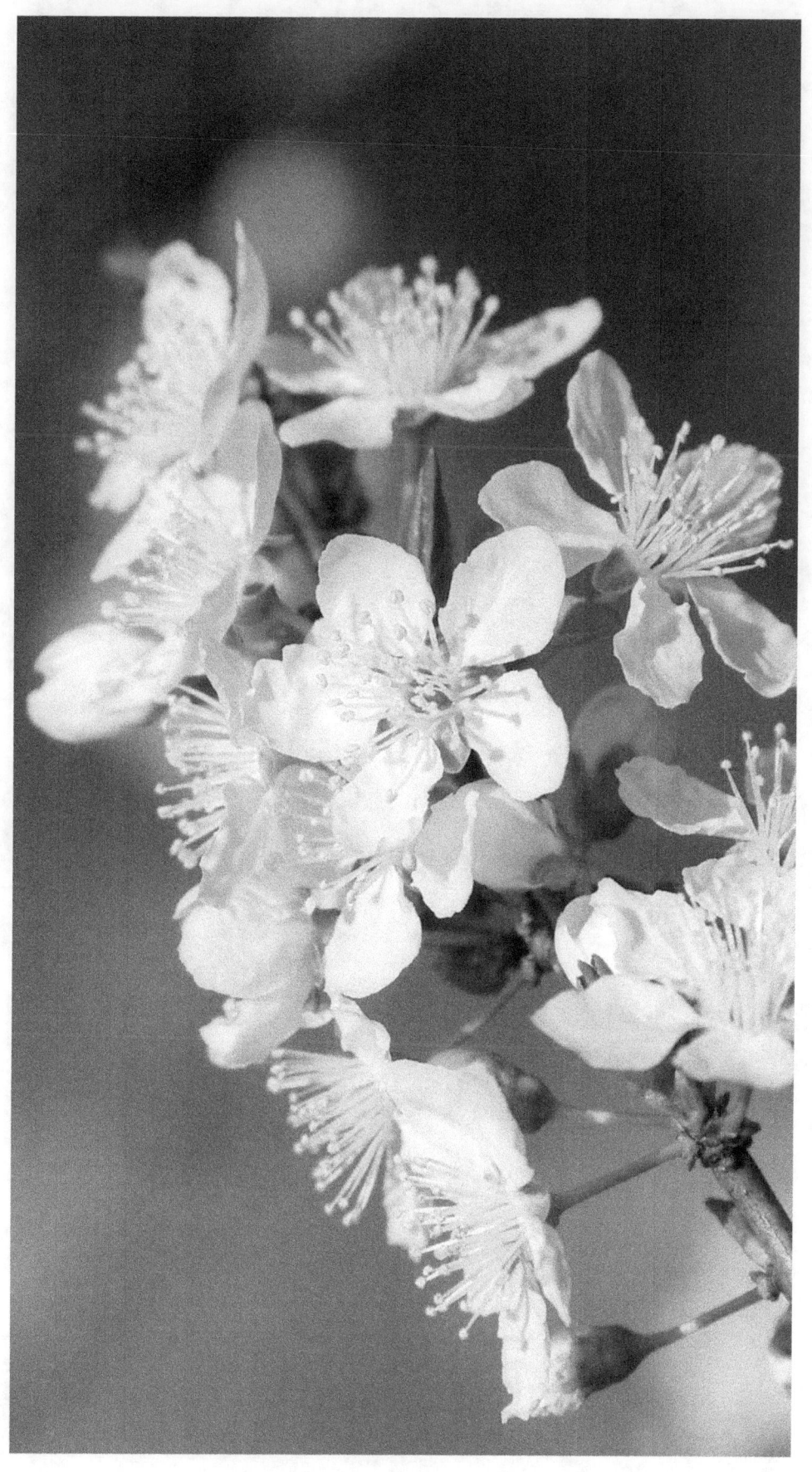

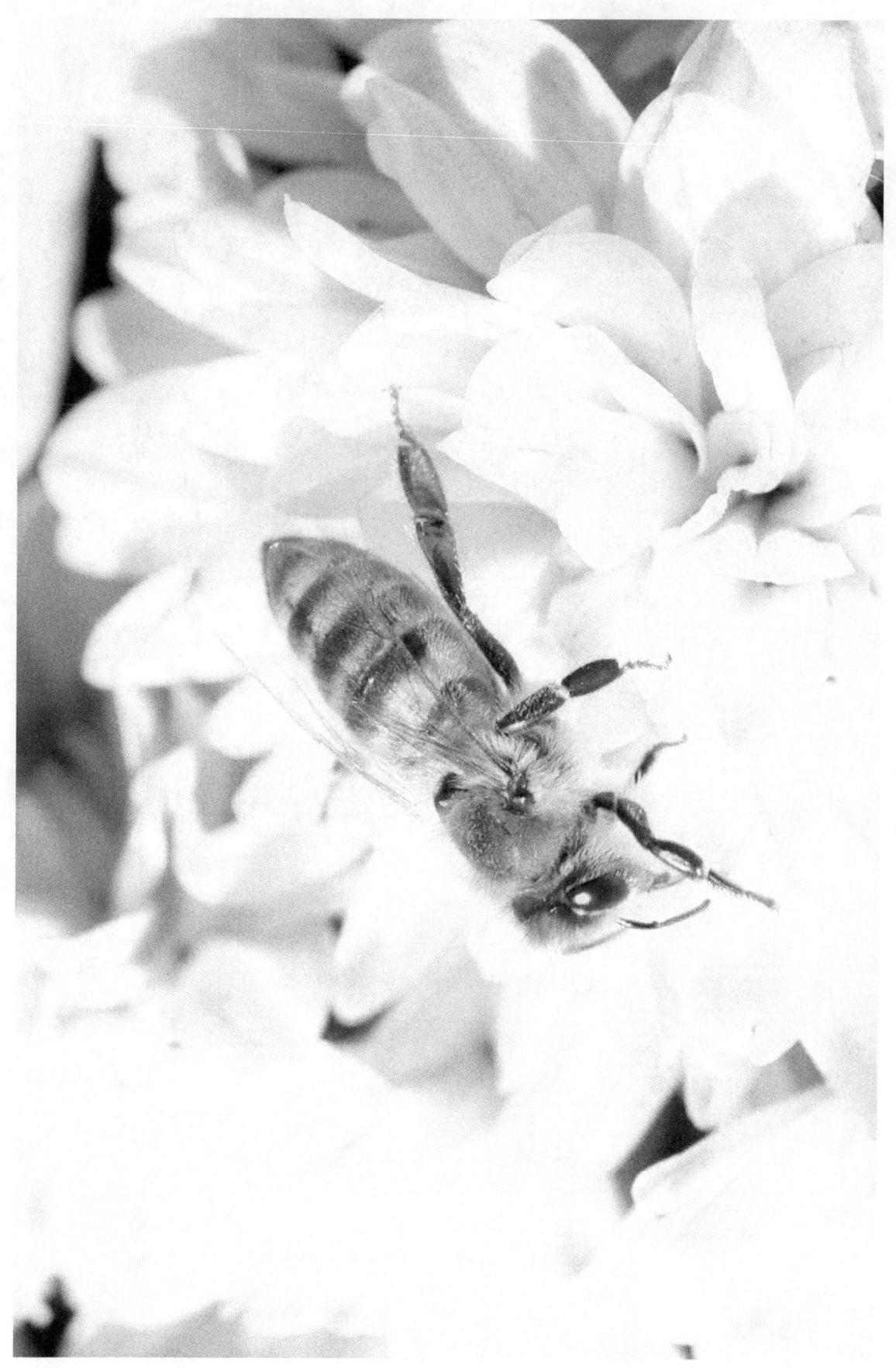

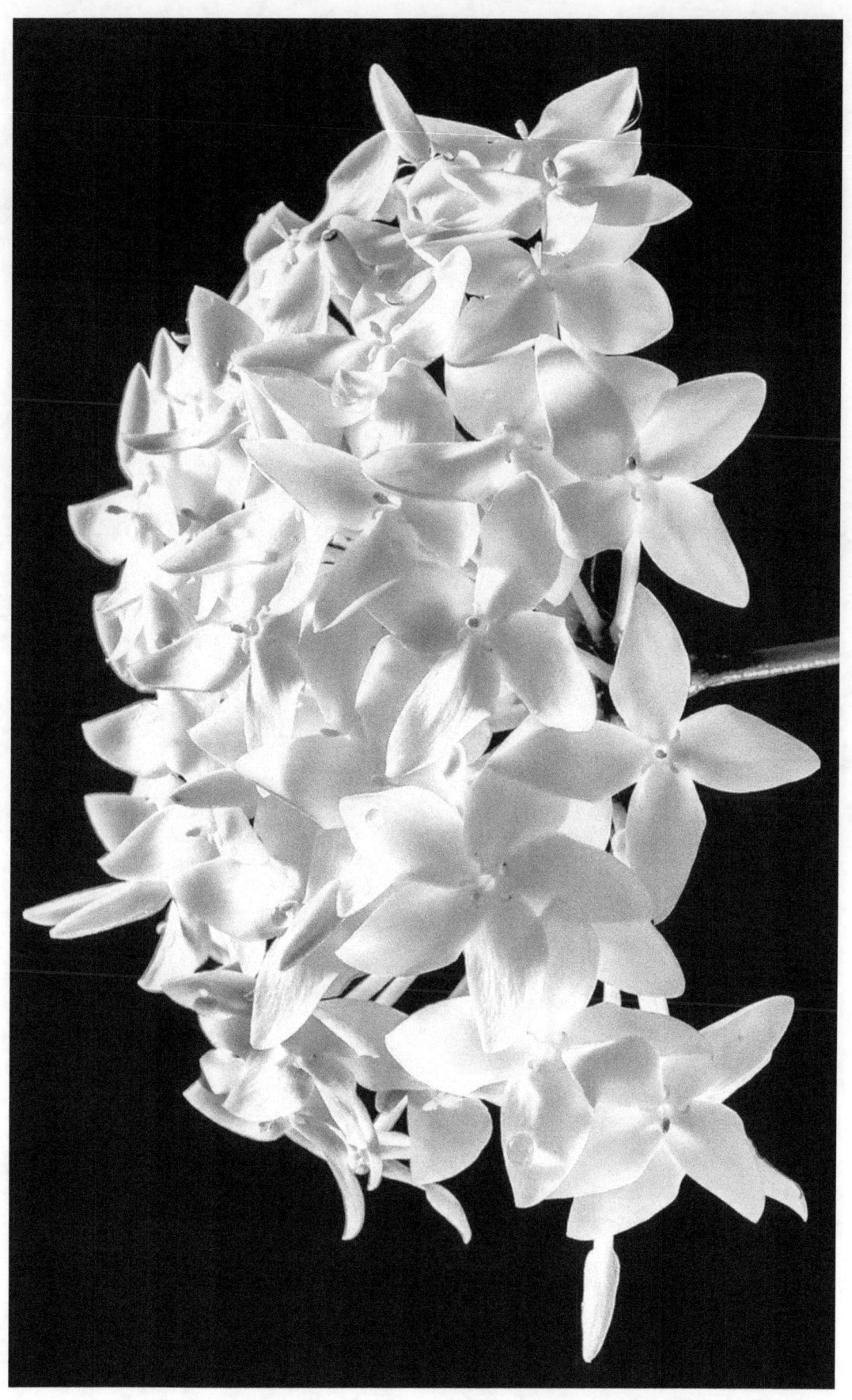

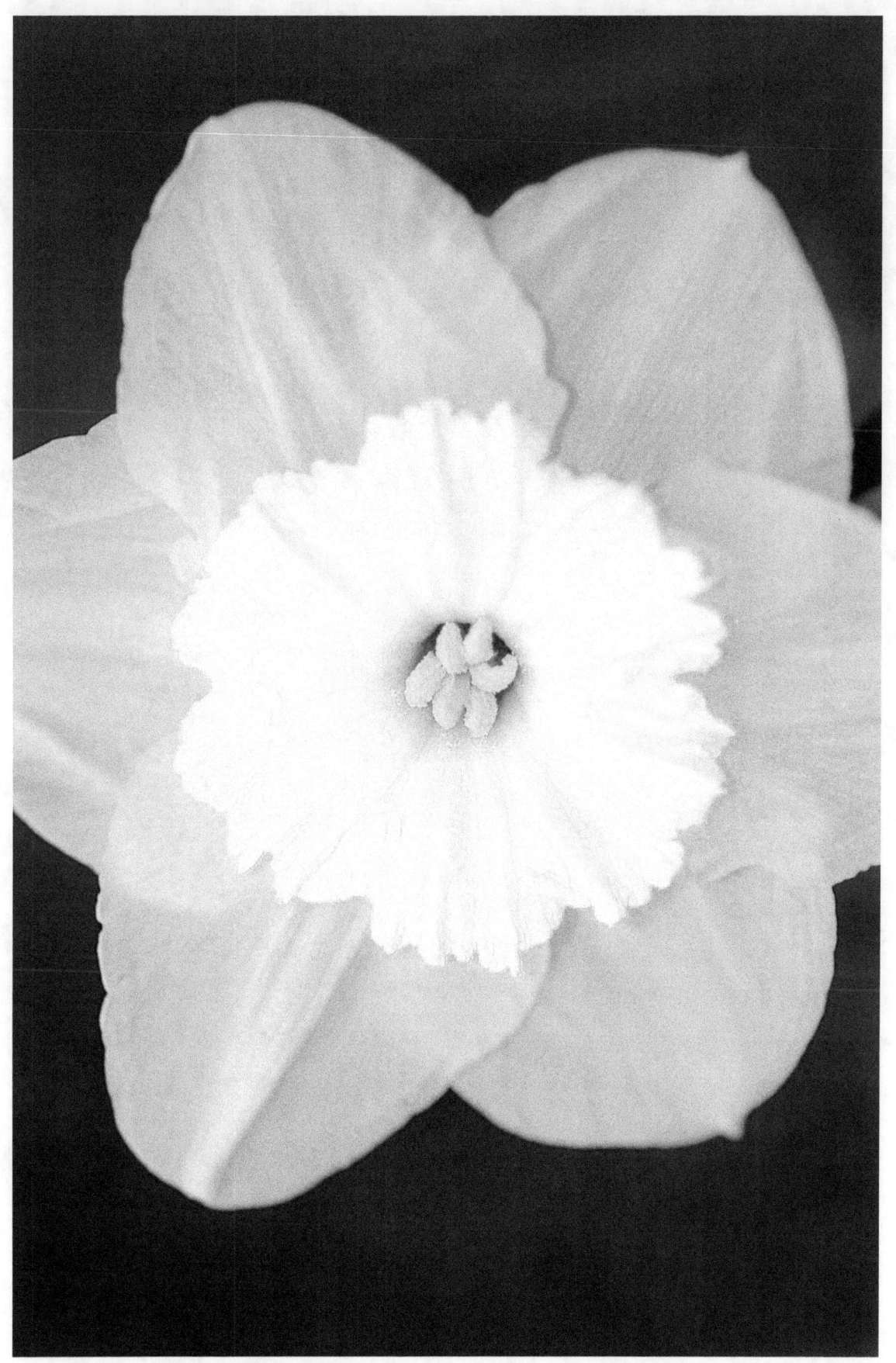

www.ingramcontent.com/pod-product-compliance
Lightning Source LLC
Chambersburg PA
CBHW080546190526
45169CB00007B/2663